CHASING
Lewis & Clark
ACROSS AMERICA

A 21ˢᵗ Century Aviation Adventure

CHASING
Lewis & Clark
ACROSS AMERICA

A 21st Century Aviation Adventure

Ron Lowery and Mary Walker

WINDSOCK MEDIA
ADVENTURE in 360°

At the entrance to one of the most dramatic places in the Columbia River Gorge, at The Dalles, a rich panorama unfolds before us as we climb over a high ridge that resembles the wrinkled skin on an elephant's back.

For information:
Windsock Media
6303 Clark Road
Harrison, Tennessee 37341 USA
423.344.3701

Library of Congress Control Number: 2004103058
ISBN 0-9749207-1-1

Photographs, Captions and Photographer's Notes: Ron Lowery
Text: Mary Walker
Designer: Sue Lowery
Editor: Rich Bailey
Printed in China
by C&C Offset Printing Co., LTD

First Edition
For information about art prints from these pictures
WWW.CHASINGLEWISANDCLARK.COM
423.344.3701

WINDSOCK MEDIA
ADVENTURE in 360°

www.windsockmedia.com

Foreword

As a longtime aviator, aircraft builder, and aspiring writer, I can fully relate to the efforts and accomplishments of Ron Lowery and Mary Walker in this wonderful work of theirs. Further, deprived of my freedom and the opportunity to fly, for the nearly six and a half years I spent in the prisons of North Vietnam, I may have a unique perspective on the many joys and "psychic income" associated with flying over and photographing any area of this marvelous land we call "home."

Perhaps the principal reason most pilots give for choosing to fly is their hunger to relish the visual feast seen only from on high. Flying is always a special experience for us but, frankly, some flights are more rewarding than others. My wife and I have flown much of the same beautiful scenery. Our views too were spectacular, but they lacked the intimacy and ability to safely linger and appreciate afforded by *Cloud Chaser* to its crew.

As Ron has captured the scenic color of the chase in his masterful images of landscape and river, so Mary has artfully woven their experiences and the local, close-up "color" of people and events into a tapestry of words befitting and complementing a visual story of this magnitude. Together they have created a book unique among photo books, one that treats the reader both to a remarkable visual experience and a fascinating adventure story. Their collaboration and teamwork have brought about a beautifully blended example of how one plus one can often equal much more than "two."

This story captures your imagination, and whisks you away on a present-day journey and celebration through reflections of the past. In the process, it will add color and life to, and more clearly define, whatever understanding you may already have had of the magnificent adventure of Lewis and Clark. I would be surprised if you did not, much like me, come away from the experience saying, "Wow—I wish I had done that!"

—*Commander Allan R. Carpenter*

Editor's note:
Commander Allan R. "Al" Carpenter, U.S. Navy(Retired), flew A-4E Skyhawk light-attack aircraft during two combat deployments to the war in Vietnam. He was shot down twice, lastly on Nov. 1, 1966, in North Vietnam, where he was captured and held until March 4, 1973. Following repatriation, he completed his 23-year Navy career and went on to pursue various interests in civilian (general) aviation. He remains an active flyer, with more than 6,000 hours total flight time, to date.

In a theater called "Planet Earth" I sit in a balcony seat narrower than a canoe. With nothing below me but the air we breathe, I become a witness to artistry created by eons of change. Despite a large wing and two powerful engines behind me, a feeling of serenity surrounds me. The simplicity of perching with barely enough room for flight instruments and camera bonds me emotionally to the plot of the show.

Since the theater is round, the show runs continuously. With the control stick in hand, I interact with the scenes. Reducing power and lowering flaps is like putting the show into slow motion. Pivoting on my wingtip, I can rerun the scene.

As new vistas unfold beneath me, I raise the camera. How can I possibly capture the grandeur of all I see before me? Although beauty abounds, I'll have to be very selective in my composition. My mind analyzes what my eyes have seen. Suddenly the elements come together—the curve of the river, the morning mist around the trees, hay bales randomly placed in the fields. As I bank to the right, the low morning sun throws rays of light through the cottonwoods and the river takes on hues from yellow to blue.

The plane flies, but it's my mind that soars.

—Ron Lowery

Contents

CHAPTER ONE
Origins of an Odyssey 10

CHAPTER TWO
Sky Road to Adventure 20

CHAPTER THREE
Rising on the High Plains 30

CHAPTER FOUR
Flying the Missouri Breaks 52

CHAPTER FIVE
Threshold of the Rockies 72

CHAPTER SIX
Challenge of the Mountains 86

CHAPTER SEVEN
Descent Into the Unknown 98

CHAPTER EIGHT
Columbia River Passage to the Sea 116

CHAPTER NINE
Homeward Bound: Then and Now 136

CHAPTER TEN
In the Red-Haired Doctor's Town 154

Near Glendive, Montana

Preface

In June 2003 we set out across America in a green "canoe in the sky" to retrace the journey of Lewis and Clark's Corps of Discovery. We modern-day adventurers—a pilot/photographer and a pilot/writer—traveled in a homebuilt, open-cockpit airplane, navigating our way over great cities and mighty rivers. The winds of the western plains had their go at us. The high mountain passes dared us to cross. We began our trip from a soggy, rain-soaked St. Louis, and by the time we returned three months later, we had logged more than 14,000 miles and nearly 200 hours in the cockpit of the slow-flying Cloud Chaser.

From our aerial platform, Ron Lowery photographed some of the most beautiful terrain in the world. We lifted off before sunrise, sometimes from a rugged dirt strip, to witness the play of first light on rivers, on rugged mountains and canyons, on cliffs and ocean beaches. We floated for hours over fields of grain and reveled in the abundance of the land. Our versatile little plane climbed high enough for the camera to capture the form and function of landscapes and low enough to let us smell the mud in the rivers and the flax in the fields.

Following the trail of history proved to be a great way to structure an adventure. We found traces of the epic explorers on riverbanks and the Pacific shore. Best of all, we found Americans celebrating their past while designing a future filled with hope.

Ron challenged himself to create ever more perfect compositions from his nimble airborne tripod. In my role as writer, I knocked on doors and gave myself license to ask innumerable questions. We found ways to enter the lives of people of all heritages and occupations—natives and settlers, fishermen and cropduster pilots.

Our journey has rewarded us with a wealth of memories and a profound love for our country and its people. We hope this story of our odyssey will open doors of adventure and wonder for everyone who reads it.

—Mary Walker

CHAPTER ONE

Origins of an Odyssey

"CLEAR," RON YELLS. HE TOGGLES THE SWITCH TO START the left engine. In the chill of the morning air it shudders and shakes like a sleeping dragon. "Just takes a little coaxing," Ron says over the intercom. Suddenly the prop roars to life. The second engine starts immediately. Within seconds, both are humming smoothly.

Ron and I are buckled in. His camera and lenses are stowed within easy reach of the front seat, my notepad and pen are in the pocket in front of me. We request clearance to depart. "Niner-four-four-romeo-lima, taxi to runway 12," the controller replies.

Ron requests runway four instead, because it's a shorter taxi and will point us toward downtown St. Louis. "Taxi to four," says the controller, "but do you realize runway four is only 3,000 feet long?"

"We only need a hundred feet," Ron answers, an amazingly short distance for a takeoff. "A hundred?" the controller exclaims, and we think we hear laughter in the control tower before the radio goes quiet. Ron says to me over the intercom, "Ready? Let's show them the homesick angel routine!"

He pushes the throttles forward, and in five seconds our wheels lift off the ground. In 60 seconds, we climb to 2,000 feet. We've taken a giant leap into the sky in *Cloud Chaser,* an oddly-shaped flying machine with diaphanous wings. "Maintain visual separation from the Arch," the controller warns. Some barnstorming blood runs through most pilots' veins, so he must know how tempting it is to slip a small plane through the silvery Gateway Arch.

Today, St. Charles revels in its colorful, historic background. Cars fill its cobblestone streets, and a bevy of festivals, including the Fleur-De-Lis Festival, celebrate its French roots.

Images of America: Lantern Slide Collection; Courtesy of the Frances Loeb Library, Graduate School of Design, Harvard University

An engraving shows St. Louis fifty years after Lewis and Clark set off from this fur-trading town into the "Great Unknown."

ST. LOUIS, MISSOURI

Approaching St. Louis from the east, with the morning sun behind us, the shining Gateway Arch is a beckoning invitation to go west.
The city stands at the confluence of the two magnificent rivers of the nation, the Mississippi and the Missouri.

After completing the preflight inspection, I pause for a moment with my hand resting on the plane's tail structure. In the distance, the glowing Gateway Arch and the St. Louis skyline rise above the ground fog. We're surrounded on the downtown airport ramp by all types of certified aircraft, all with skins tougher than my homebuilt plane, *Cloud Chaser*. Each one has millions of time-proven miles in their designs. They've no doubt earned the right to sit there looking smug. In this last moment before we set out on our own voyage of discovery, I ponder the fate of my hand-sculpted creation of fabric and aluminum with its comparatively few miles of flight.

It's been more than three years since *Cloud Chaser* emerged from its birthplace in a hangar in Sebring, Florida. Since then, more than 650 hours have been entered in its logbook. Most of those

Cloud Chaser *floats over the Missouri River, barely above the treetops.*

hours, however, have been two- to three-hour photo flights after which the plane returned to its hangar for shelter from the elements.

Cloud Chaser's main goal has always been to explore and photograph the world. Well, today it's time to truly prove its worth. For the next three months, it won't be sleeping behind the security of those 12-foot hangar doors. Will Mother Nature be merciful and provide safe passage through tornado alley in the Midwest? Will a hailstorm pound it to the ground or ferocious winds rip it from its moorings at night?

Facing the gateway to the west I wonder... when we return months from now, will the plane be a trailer full of aircraft parts? Or will we and *Cloud Chaser* emerge from the wilderness tempered by the fire of adventure and bearing the photographic and personal testimony we seek?

Time to stop pondering and let the adventure begin.

In the soft mist of dawn, we're strapped into a diminutive airplane no wider than a canoe, starting the adventure we've been planning for two years. Flying low and slow in a homebuilt open-cockpit plane, we'll retrace the epic journey of Lewis and Clark one airborne step at a time.

The elegant Arch stands at the edge of the Mississippi River in a spacious park that spreads out at the base of the city like a welcome mat. Nestled just behind it is the Old Courthouse, built only 30 years after the passage of Meriwether Lewis and William Clark. St. Louis was a small trading post in 1803 when the explorers camped near here at Wood River to assemble their Corps of Discovery. Then, the town of about 1,000 residents was a small outpost on the frontier. The Captains could not have imagined the explosion of technology and commerce that has molded this riverport city, and our nation, over the past two hundred years.

From the sky, we can see how the pieces of the modern city fit together. Circling slowly at 1,800 feet, we have a hawk's eye view of the riverfront and the core of downtown St. Louis. The stores and factories are closed at this early hour, but a casino riverboat glows with neon colors on the east bank of the river. Just a few pedestrians and cars move on the quiet morning streets.

Our curiosity dictates where we turn, what scenes we explore. To fly this freely across a free land is a joyful experience and an incredible privilege—one unknown in most parts of the world.

Wind in Our Faces, Bugs in Our Teeth

Cloud Chaser is an Experimental Class airplane originally designed for a National Geographic project to photograph the African Congo. The pilot/photographer sits way out in front of the wing, so he can shoot wide angles without a wingtip, strut or gear leg getting in the picture. The plane can fly low and slow, with a stall speed of 35 mph, but it can climb "like a rocket" at 1,800 feet per minute, allowing Ron to grab a high-altitude shot or quickly get out of a tight situation. An eight-foot tail gives stability, and the redundancy and reliability of the twin engines provide a huge safety factor.

A curious deer in a wetlands near Onawa, Iowa.

When Ron saw the prototype plane in 1996, he knew it was the perfect platform for his aerial photography and exploration. He and his older son, Alan, built *Cloud Chaser* from a kit in 2000. Although the Experimental classification may give pause to the uninitiated, the plane had to meet rigorous engineering and construction specifications, and the design has been tested and proven in exceptionally rugged conditions. With its open-cockpit design, *Cloud Chaser* is often mistaken for an Ultralight, despite its wingspan of 36 feet and length of 27 feet from nose to tail. However, weighing in at 1,054 pounds and boasting two 100 horsepower engines, it is considerably beyond the Ultralight Class, which tops out at 250 pounds and 60 horsepower. The plane has plenty of power to soar to high altitudes. Ron often climbs to 13,000 feet to take photos above the clouds. He suspects he could go to 24,000 feet, but no one has tested the plane beyond 18,000.

Climbing into the cockpit demands a maneuver worthy of an intermediate yoga student: grab a wing strut with one hand, step up on a wheel strut with one foot and reach the other leg across the seat and down into a slim well, put weight on that leg, then swing the torso into the seat. The shallow aluminum shell of the fuselage comes only up to seat height, so we are perched up higher than the sidewalls, as in a canoe. The airframe sits low to the ground. When we're on the ramp, my fingertips can almost brush the runway.

We are strapped in with heavy-duty shoulder harnesses hooked to the wings and seat belts attached to the frame. The wings are high up behind us, made of Dacron fabric fitted over a latticework of aluminum tubes. The two engines are mounted on the trailing edges of the wings, out of the way for photography. I wear ski goggles to shield my eyes from the wind, and my bright blue helmet has a built-in intercom so I can communicate with Ron.

Flying in *Cloud Chaser* is like no other aviation experience I've had. With two engines on a lightweight body, every takeoff is like a fast elevator ride into the sky. When we settle into cruise, we're on a magic carpet, turning and banking freely, in touch with the air around us, able to smell the river below. Flying in the open air is the airborne equivalent of a motorcycle ride, with the wind stinging our cheeks. When we landed after my first ride in *Cloud Chaser,* Ron asked, "Did you get bugs in your teeth?"

Our Journey of Discovery

We intend to spend three months along the famous Lewis and Clark trail capturing both the essence of history and the flavor of modern life from an aerial perspective. We have left behind jobs and homes, families and commitments, to chase after spectacular photographs and an adventure tale.

Ron's wife, Sue, hands him a telephoto lens as he prepares for a photo flight from St. Louis Downtown Airport in Cahokia, Illinois.

We'll freely borrow all the courage, determination and resourcefulness we can from the Corps of Discovery. Lewis, Clark and company set the standard when they rowed and poled the Missouri River upstream against the current, portaged boats around giant waterfalls and crossed mountain ranges that arose in defiance where maps showed only blank spaces.

Ron is our photographer, chief pilot and cheerful morale booster. He's challenging himself to capture images of the slow dance of river and terrain, the interplay of natural and man-made patterns on the land and water. He wants to show how rivers are, at the same time, the sculptors of landscape and the arteries of the nation, pulsing through farms and forests, communities and cities.

I'm the writer, Lewis and Clark amateur historian, and backup pilot. As roving journalist for our expedition, I want to engage readers in our tremendous voyage of discovery. I'm eager to scout each new place, to meet the people who live on the land and to learn about their histories and their dreams for the future. As Ron searches for colorful tapestries of visual elements, I'll look for the rich complexity of human communities.

Ron has flown *Cloud Chaser* from the Lowerys' home in Chattanooga, and I've driven an RV from my home in Tucson with a friend who will be part of our ground crew for a few weeks. Ron's wife Sue and son Ryan round out the team. They've driven a diesel pickup pulling a fifth-wheel camper from Chattanooga.

We want to follow the footsteps of Lewis and Clark—but on our own terms. We'll use satellite photos to plan our route and satellite signals to navigate it, a far cry from following the sketchy and speculative maps of 200 years ago. We'll fly over rivers and mountains that the Corps of Discovery painstakingly traversed at ground level. Our plane and campers afford us freedom and protection, but we suspect the elements might still find ways to break through our high tech defenses.

On the Trail at Last

After several days of being grounded by rain, Ron and I are glad to be started on our own voyage of discovery. Climbing and cruising past downtown, the Way West is calling us.

We salute the Gateway Arch with a waggle of wings, point the plane north toward the mouth of the Missouri River, and head upstream along the eastern bank of the Mississippi. Soon we are "dead reckoning" over the Missouri, navigating by reference to landmarks on the ground. It's a fresh spring morning and the "Big Muddy" is true to its nickname. The brown water smells musky, the fields are sodden.

The Missouri is the longest river in the United States, extending more than 2,500 miles including its headwater streams. Last night in camp we traced its winding blue line on a map, noting the towns it passes, the terrain and distances. Today we trace the watery highway with an airplane. The river is our trail, and we are content to go wherever it cares to take us. Every little town, every rock bluff on the riverbank is a treasure.

The cornstalks are planted in precise rows on the contoured fields, and they're only six inches tall. Against the light tan earth, the dark shoots look like the tentative hair of a new transplant on a bald man's head.

We wave to a tugboat crew, and then Ron dips low to photograph a snag in the river. "Sometimes I almost forget I have no floats on this plane," he says, "because the first airplane I built did—it could have landed on this river."

This kind of open-cockpit flying is the closest thing to the "bodily" soaring some of us do in our dreams. When we bank in a turn, nothing is between us but air and the water. When Ron raises his camera to shoot, he has an open field of vision.

While he's scanning each scene for photo possibilities, I'm wondering how he chooses his shots. Sometimes he'll circle five fields that all look very much the same to me before selecting one to photograph. "What makes that one special?" I finally ask. "It has all the right elements of an interesting composition. The sidelighting of the contours of the field complements the curve of the river," he says.

I'm trying to take notes while we're aloft, but with the air whipping my face and arms, just holding on to a pad and pen is quite a trick. My handwriting looks remarkably like my electrocardiogram, so I give it up.

Besides, I'd rather take the controls whenever I can. Sometimes I fly from the rear seat while Ron changes his camera lens, eats a snack or relaxes by listening to music on a fancy stereo that's wired into the intercoms. I'm free to cruise the right bank of the river, then the left, or go inland according to whatever catches my eye.

Up ahead is a blue-green field of soybeans bordered by a grassy chartreuse levee. Beyond that is an oxbow, a comma-shaped and tree-lined pond separated from the river. It's a curving meander that was cut off long ago when the fickle Missouri changed its course. Around every bend is a new clue about the life of the land and the water. I would happily explore the whole world like this.

River, crops and trees complement each other in an expression of America's richness.

Eyes of the Nation

When Lewis and Clark were preparing for their journey, the treaty that had officially ratified the independence of the United States of America was a mere 20 years old. The nation consisted of 17 states near the Atlantic seacoast, and the Mississippi River formed the western boundary of the country. The United States was a vulnerable new player in the arena of world politics. The threat of foreign control of the Mississippi River and the vast lands reaching westward beyond it meant that the United States' toehold on the continent was tenuous and its survival as a nation uncertain.

President Jefferson had sent envoys to Napoleon Bonaparte in Paris to try to purchase the critically important port of New Orleans, through which half of all U.S. trade goods already passed. In the spring of 1803, fate handed the fledgling United States a great gift of good fortune.

Napoleon needed hard cash to conduct his European wars, he was having difficulty controlling his Caribbean colonies, and he could not spare troops to secure the North American lands owned by France. He suddenly offered the U.S. the entire Louisiana Territory—about 820,000 square miles—for three cents an acre. Although the purchase price of $15 million exceeded the country's annual federal budget, Jefferson boldly closed the deal. By this master-stroke, he doubled the size of the young nation, secured New Orleans and gained control of the center of the continent. Had events turned out differently, two-thirds of the present United States might have remained in foreign hands.

The visionary Jefferson had long advocated a grand exploration across the continent. Now, with the ink on the Louisiana Purchase barely dry, he instructed Meriwether Lewis and William Clark to become the eyes and ears of a nation hungry for knowledge about the new territory that had just doubled its size.

America's economic future hinged on becoming competitive with Britain in the northwest fur trade and establishing a commercial route westward across the continent to the Pacific Ocean. The U.S. vitally needed to gain information about the geography and resources of the new territory it had just acquired and to develop alliances with the Indian tribes who resided there.

An engraving of Meriwether Lewis in Shoshone Indian Dress

On the Pacific shore, the mouth of the Columbia River had been charted, but a practicable water/land route across the continent—the long-sought Northwest Passage—had yet to be found. The geography of the Rocky Mountains was unknown, and rumor had it that prehistoric beasts and red-haired Indians of Welsh descent lived in the wild lands around them.

With the newly formed Corps of Discovery, a crew consisting of 35 soldiers, Clark's slave York and a team of French boatmen, Captains Lewis and Clark started upstream on the Missouri River in May 1804 to provide what the nation lacked— a realistic view of the continent. They would dare to explore the foreign-claimed lands west of the Continental Divide, beyond the new boundary of the United States.

So began one of the world's great journeys of exploration, adventure and accomplishment. With fortitude, resourcefulness, a bit of luck and the kindness of strangers, the Corps prevailed over grueling terrain and harsh conditions.

While trekking some 8,000 miles across North America and back, Lewis and Clark created astoundingly accurate maps and detailed journals that became the basis of the nation's scientific, commercial and cultural knowledge of the West. President Jefferson wrote, "Never did a similar event excite more joy through the United States. The humblest of its citizens had taken a lively interest in the issue of this journey, and looked forward with impatience for the information it would furnish."

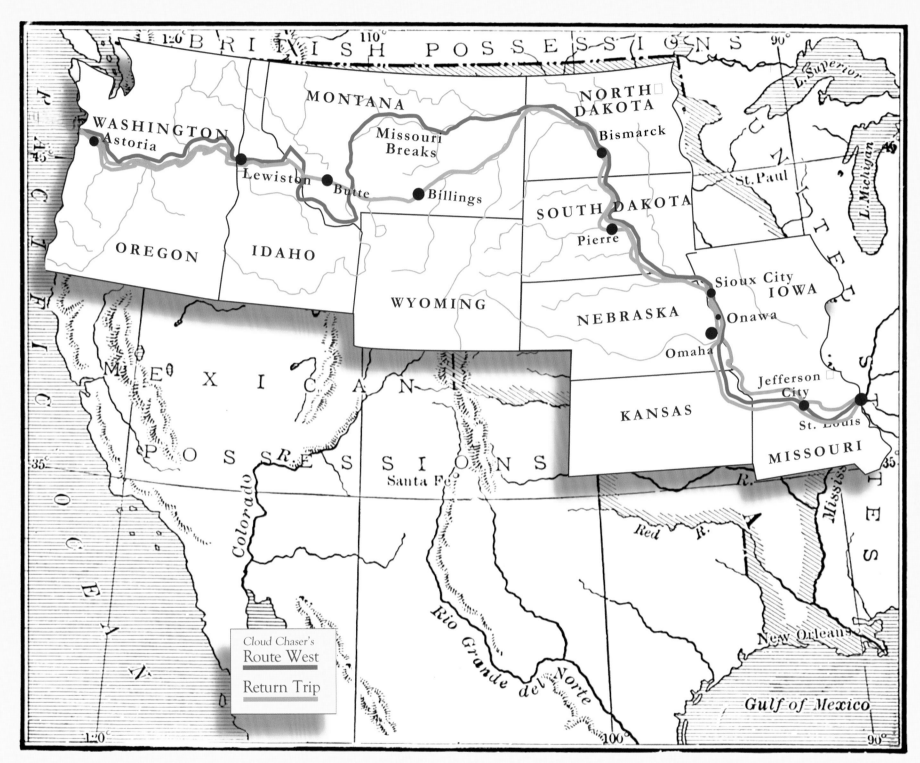

Starting in St. Louis, our route followed closely the Corp of Discovery's path.

GRAIN VALLEY, MISSOURI

Like echoes of the undulating Missouri River, contoured rows of crops surround these farm buildings.
Do these farmers take art classes?

GRAIN VALLEY, MISSOURI

In the morning mist, the Missouri is a river of gold that appears to flow from the rising sun.
The oxbows are snapshots of the river's past, now fading like the hoof-prints of the buffalo.

Sky Road to Adventure

LEWIS AND CLARK WOULD HAVE LOVED THE comfortable ride we are enjoying in our "flying canoe." On this lower portion of the Missouri, the explorers labored hard to cover at most 14 miles each day. Their boats continually ran aground on sandbars, got twisted in snags and mired in mud. The winds were often so strong that the Corps had to resort to cordelling—tying ropes to the boats and pulling them from the shore. Crossing the present-day state of Missouri took them six weeks.

The river is much different now. From the sky we have a clear view of how dams and levees have changed the lower Missouri. Until about 50 years ago, the Missouri would chew its banks for breakfast and create new ones by noon. It would spread out in a mile-wide braided pattern of small channels, islands and sandbars so storm waters and springtime snowmelt could slowly dissipate.

In many places the stream is channelized now— confined between rigid walls or levees to reduce the flooding of towns and fields. But barriers that solve problems in one area cause flooding upstream, where the water is forced to pool, and downstream, where it flows in rapid torrents. Before such controls the river simply spread out wherever it chose and the waters were absorbed gradually. In his book *River Horse*, William Least Heat-Moon wrote that the Osage Indians have no word in their native language for "flood."

True to its name, the "Big Muddy" cuts a path through rich farm land. Along the banks, erratic patterns of young green sprouts reach for the early summer sun while absorbing the remnants of the latest heavy rains.

JEFFERSON CITY, MISSOURI

Following the Missouri River's twists and turns through the bottomland, suddenly the state capitol looms into view above the cornfields
like a great white temple. It's crowned with a bronze statue of the Roman goddess Ceres, patroness of grain.

"Floods are white man's things," he was told. River management is now being re-evaluated, with an eye toward restoring floodplains and wetlands in some areas to control floods more naturally and to increase fish and wildlife habitat.

Beyond a railroad bridge at Glasgow we see seven barges and two tugs docked at the river's edge and, further along, a sand dredge. Huge grain elevators dominate the small town, seeming out of scale, as if someone has set oversized blocks from the wrong toy box next to tiny houses in a model railroad layout. Beyond the few streets near the river, farmhouses are staggered at greater and greater intervals stretching 50 miles to the horizon.

High Spirits in Kansas City

We land at the small East Kansas City Airport at Grain Valley, Missouri. The airport has one general aviation service company, called a "fixed-base operator" or FBO in aviation parlance, that provides fuel and services for private aircraft and small corporate planes. Here we find a typical FBO, with a staff of two or three people who are eager to help pilots and passengers in every way. A lobby, an office and a pilots' lounge with recliners for quick naps during layovers are inside.

"Hangar rats" are another feature of most small FBOs—retired aviation buffs who hang around, swapping stories and watching planes come and go. This afternoon when our ground crew pulls up with the RV campers, one of the hangar rats comes to our aid. He hops in his car and leads us to a nearby campground.

In the evening Ron and Sue set out to do a photo flight, but first they must refuel *Cloud Chaser*. The plane is particular about the type of gas it sips. The lead in aviation fuel doesn't agree with the ROTAX engines, causing lead buildup in the engine parts. The premium unleaded automobile variety that the plane prefers is not available at airports, so Ron mounted a custom fuel tank for it in the back of the diesel truck that pulls his fifth-wheel camper. With this arrangement he can refuel the plane anywhere and anytime—a necessity for the odd hours we often keep, flying

Lewis and Clark stood on the small green park area in the foreground—the present day Clark Point—and commented to their men that it was, "...a hill which appeared to have a Commanding Situation for a fort...."

before dawn or near sunset to get the best light for photography. *Cloud Chaser* can fly for six hours on 28 gallons of gas, making it very economical to operate.

It's a magical night for a romantic flight. The evening air is so smooth that Ron and Sue feel like they're dangling from a string. Beneath them the river flows quietly onward, connecting places and eras of history. Making a pass over the suburbs, they can see men out cutting the grass, kids playing baseball. Shade trees cast long shadows across lush lawns.

In camp after the flight, our crew gathers around to celebrate Ryan's 19th birthday. We're "in high Spirits," just like the Corps, who often passed the long evenings entertaining themselves and Native American guests with "verry lively Danceing & Singing &c.," according to Clark's journals. We make our own music on mountain dulcimer, harmonica and spoons, and then sing along with recordings of *Soldier's Joy* and other folk songs that the Corps might have known.

Chasing on the Ground

Morning finds us touring Kansas City with five people and a dog in Ron's truck, and "Chasing Lewis and Clark" takes on new meaning. Ron and I pride ourselves on our pilot-trained senses of direction, but the site of the Corp's encampment eludes us. We cross the Missouri three times and the Kansas twice before we give up.

Lewis wrote that he camped "... in the point above the Kansas River," but historians aren't sure of the exact location. From the air we saw a wooded point of land where the two rivers join, but it turns out to be bounded by an industrial area with no public access. It seems that the cities on both sides of the Missouri turned their backs on the river during their industrial growth spurts. Now they're funding major projects to showcase the waterways and beautify bridges, but the Corp's campsite is still obscure.

Next we search for Clark Point, an advertised landmark of the Corps of Discovery. After asking directions several times, we succeed. On a hilltop

KANSAS CITY, KANSAS

Kansas City, one of America's industrial giants, is the last large city we will encounter during the next two months.

overlooking the Missouri, we find a small park with a handsome bronze sculpture of the Captains, Sacagawea and her infant son, and Lewis' dog Seaman.

Taking to the air again in the evening for sunset shots, Ron and I don't lose our way. As we circle the city several times at 40 mph—a crawling pace for an airplane—the air traffic controller comes on the radio to ask, "What are you moving that thing with, pedal power?"

To get the shot of Clark Point that Ron wants, we need to circle just off the runway of the downtown airport. This takes a great deal of coordination with the tower controller, who does his best to let us maneuver into the position we want, in between the arrival and departure of other aircraft. I gladly take the controls, watch for planes, monitor the radio and fly tight circles while Ron tries to shoot the handkerchief-sized park.

Snow Globe Towns

Flying out of Kansas City in the morning, the freeway junctions are busy and flowing with energy below us. The river makes a right angle bend here, and we follow it upstream for many miles until it becomes the border between Nebraska and Iowa. The soil looks dark and rich. Neat farmhouses and tiny towns are scattered across the cultivated fields like scenes in snow globes, vignettes of perfection.

Lewis and Clark had encountered small groups of Indians frequently along their route, but their first formal council was with six or seven chiefs of the Missouri and Oto tribes near the present town of Council Bluffs, which was named in honor of the historic event. Here the Captains established a format they would use for many meetings with tribal leaders further along the trail. They erected the main sail of the keelboat as an awning to provide shade. In the heat of an August day, Corps members marched in wool uniforms and full military regalia. Lewis astonished the natives by shooting his air gun—an unusual air rifle that could be fired repeatedly without recharging. The Captains informed the chiefs they were now children of a great new father in Washington who desired for them to live in peace and to trade with no other nation but the United States.

Fort Osage, near present-day Sibley, Missouri, was the first U.S. fort to be built within the Louisiana Purchase lands. It functioned as one of the first military outposts and government trade houses in the Purchase. Built under William Clark's direction in 1808 as Fort Sibley, it was later renamed for the Osage Indians. In the late evening light, the restored fort is eerily empty.

Ahead of the Storm

At sunset we land at one of the smallest airports in the country, at Onawa, Iowa, having escaped dark gray thunderheads building behind us to the south. The runway edge is a newly mown hayfield. Ron pulls off the concrete, and we dig out the tie-down rings, which are buried six inches deep in rich Iowa loam, weeds and hay. We don't see another aircraft in sight. Maybe we're the only visitors this summer.

We camp at Lewis and Clark State Park, build a fire and sing until midnight with a local music teacher from the next campsite. Our campground has showers with hot water here, but you have to push a button outside the stall to get a timed amount of water. "Seems like the government has figured out exactly how much water you need to take a shower and shave," says Ron, "and they figured wrong."

Keelboat Dreams

A full-scale replica of Lewis and Clark's keelboat floats on an oxbow lake at the park, and it's the second replica of the Corps of Discovery's flagship we've seen. The 55-foot keelboat traveled with two smaller pirogues from the mouth of the Missouri to the Mandan Villages in North Dakota.

We first saw a keelboat replica in a handsome new boathouse at the river's edge in St. Charles, Missouri. Members of a group called the Discovery Expedition built the St. Charles boat, and they sail it on the Missouri, reenacting the Corps' journey. Docking at towns along the way, they give kids and grownups "living history" lessons they'll never forget. Members of the crew tell about the challenges the Corps of Discovery met with teamwork and determination while they rowed, poled and pulled the unwieldy beast of a boat upriver for more than 1,300 miles. The reenactors are passionate about their roles. They find personal meanings in the history they explore, and they pass their enthusiasm on to others.

Boatwright A. C. "Butch" Bouvier and another group of energetic volunteers, the Friends of Discovery, completed the construction of the Iowa replica in 1991. They named their keelboat *Discovery,* although Lewis and Clark never named their craft.

The Iowa keelboat has a flat bottom, but the one built in St. Charles has a v-shaped hull. The actual hull design of Lewis' boat is one of the many unsolved mysteries of the Lewis and Clark Expedition, and the question is hotly debated among rival replica builders. The controversy has all of the force of the fourteenth century argument about whether the earth was round or flat.

The volunteer crewmen of the *Discovery* are proud to show off their handiwork, and they invite us to join them for a ride on the lake. The lumbering keelboat has no onboard motor, so a small motorboat is used to maneuver it in the manner of a border collie herding an enormous sheep.

Onawa's downtown is only three blocks long, but it's as wide as an eight lane highway. T-shirts in the local grocery store proudly proclaim this Iowa town as having "the widest Main Street in America."

Five minutes out from shore, a sudden storm cloud darkens the sky, the wind whips up, and the boat begins to pitch and yaw. The rain starts falling in torrents, so we duck into the small cabin, still getting soaked by spray from the open windows. The mate pushes the tiller to one side, and we head for the dock.

Ron is frantic about *Cloud Chaser*. The plane is parked five miles away at the airport, left uncovered after an early morning flight because no storms were expected. Ron can do nothing until the boat slowly crawls to shore. Finally on land, he makes a mad dash to the airport. Thankfully the storm has gone in a different direction and the plane is safe and dry.

The rain stops as abruptly as it came, and when Ron returns, we visit with some of the Friends of Discovery on shore. Local historian William "Buffalo Bill" Sanders is wearing buckskins and buffalo hat in the heat of this muggy June day, and he has the long hair and beard to go with the backwoodsman costume.

"The Lewis and Clark journey was a great story and the greatest expedition, better than going to the moon," Bill declares. "When people went to the moon, they knew where they were going to land and all such things. These guys went into the unknown, didn't know how many Indians there were, whether they'd be friendly or not. They found 123 animals unknown to the white man, including the prairie dog, antelope, bighorn sheep and the magpie bird. They discovered 186 different plant species, charted and mapped rivers and mountains, so it was the greatest expedition this country has ever undertaken, bar none."

Our first "council" with a Native American is with Bob Morris, a farmer and member of the Omaha Nation and a descendant of Chief Black Bird and Chief Yellow Smoke. Bob is glad that the Bicentennial is providing an opportunity for Native Americans to tell their history and to share their perspectives on the future.

Reenactor Jerry Hebenstreit wears the red, white and blue military uniform that soldiers of the Corps of Discovery donned for formal meetings with Indian chiefs. The reenactors come from all walks of life. They are doctors, lawyers, and "just plain time-clock punchers" like Jerry.

Bob says that settlers who followed on the heels of Lewis and Clark often took land that had been set aside for the Omahas but that neither his ancestors nor the squatters fully understood what was happening throughout a century of conflict because they weren't informed or educated. "You know it's very important to view both sides at the time and how they felt," says Bob. "Education is the key to helping everyone work together now." He's a proud American who wouldn't want to live anywhere else in the world.

North of Souix City the Missouri River enjoys its last taste of freedom before being tamed to follow a rigid pathway to the sea.

ONAWA, IOWA

At sunrise, the keelboat replica Discovery, *built by the group Friends of Lewis and Clark, sets sail on an oxbow lake.*

Visitors can board this full-scale replica of the flagship of the Corps and walk the benches next to the gunwales where boatmen strained to push the boat along with 30-foot poles. A swivel cannon mounted at the bow is a copy of the largest weapon carried by the Corps. Their keelboat was outfitted with 20 oars, and it carried some 24 men in addition to numerous barrels, bales and kegs containing food provisions, tools, arms and trade goods.

SOUTH OF SIOUX CITY, IOWA
Like a drunken seamstress, the Missouri River stitches Nebraska to Iowa.

ONAWA, IOWA
Cottonwoods cast long shadows in early morning fog.

CHAPTER THREE

Rising on the High Plains

TWO AIRPORTS NEAR SIOUX CITY TAKE US FROM THE ridiculous to the sublime. The first, Graham Field, is closest to the campground we want to use. It's shown as a public airport on Ron's GPS (Global Positioning System) display, but on landing we find grass growing through two cracked concrete runways that are only 36 and 11 feet wide. Runways at public airports are required to be 60 feet wide now, so this one is truly puzzling.

In the light of the setting sun, the deserted airfield seems like a phantom of the twilight zone. Swallows nest in an office building that looks like it's been locked up for years. Pieces of rusted sheet metal in the roofs of deserted hangars creak in the slight breeze. Ron would never leave his plane here. We lift off again quickly, relieved that some mysterious vortex hasn't captured us at what we dub "the airport that doesn't exist."

The next closest airport is Martin Field, on the Nebraska side of the Missouri River. We land and find some fellows chatting while they repair and polish their planes. Reassured by such definite signs of life, we bed *Cloud Chaser* down for the night.

In the morning we find that Martin Field is truly a gem, a real contender for the Small Airport of the Year in our estimation. It's a privately owned/public-use field, meaning that it straddles the bureaucratic fence, having access to government loans but still privately owned and operated. It's a well-run mom-and-pop operation. Gene Martin started the airport with his father nearly 50 years ago, and now

Ryan, Jack, Mary and Ron pose for a quick photo in front of Cloud Chaser *at the lively and hospitable Martin Field.*

Ron's "one-man air show" entertains a group of onlookers as the local media get footage for the evening news.

Described by Clark as "bald-pated," the Loess Hills (pronounced "luss") are ancient dunes formed of fine particles of soil blown from the riverbed over eons. Many slopes are terraced in narrow ledges called "cat-steps," where the fragile loess has slumped into even horizontal ridges under the topsoil.

Sergeant Floyd's monument in Sioux City, Iowa, presides over a highway and waterway. Floyd was the only member of the Corps of Discovery to perish during the Expedition.

his wife, Ginger, and his sons help out. The grandchildren take turns washing planes and squirting each other with the hose.

Gene turns out to be a gregarious ringmaster of a guy. The walls of the small FBO office are covered with photos of him posing with visiting dignitaries, aviation heroes and local leaders. He seems to know everyone in town. In the morning he calls his friends at the local TV stations and newspapers. Soon reporters, aunts, uncles, cousins and neighbors drop by to see our "green dragonfly." Grandma Ginger comes away from her desk about three o'clock with brownies for all the kids, and it's a wonderful atmosphere. The Martins take us under their familial wings for the duration of our stay.

We learn that "Siouxland" is the catchy name for the tri-city area, a friendly place that has a three-way split personality. The mid-sized metropolis encompasses three rivers and three small cities: Sioux City, Iowa; South Sioux City, Nebraska; and North Sioux City, South Dakota. As it turns out, we camp in South Dakota, hangar the plane in Nebraska, and do most of our touring on the Iowa side.

Death and Dialog at Sioux City

On our first full day in Siouxland, the winds are 20 mph gusting to 30. Clouds stretch out across the sky, some sheared in long streaky layers, some whipped into foam. It's a good day to stay on the ground and visit the new Lewis and Clark Interpretive Center in Sioux City.

The center is outstanding, with spellbinding new animatronic figures of Clark and Lewis. As the figures gesture and address each other and the spectators, the Captains' costumes, features and even their styles of speech are portrayed as accurately as possible. Lost in imagining what these men were truly like, I whisper to Sue, "I like William's Southern accent." Just then, Clark's figure turns to rivet me with its sparkling brown eyes, unnerving me for a few seconds.

Alan Hansen, director of the center, talks with us about the death of Sergeant Charles Floyd here in 1804. Floyd was the only member of the Corps of Discovery to die during the

PICKSTOWN, SOUTH DAKOTA

We asked Joseph Lufkins, a Sisseton Wahpeton Dakota, about the significance of the markings on his face. This powwow participant laughed and answered, "It's war paint. I just use it to scare the grandkids."

expedition, of what experts now believe was a burst appendix. None of the Captains' remedies could possibly have saved him.

"Sergeant Floyd's death was a blow that could have broken up the expedition," explained Alan. "Fate had taken a hearty young man in a way that no one understood. The men could have given in to superstitious fears about the journey ahead, but Lewis and Clark's strong leadership gave them the courage to continue on the expedition. I believe that the sobering experience of burying one of their own was a key factor in forging the Corps into a single body, purposeful and determined."

The Lewis and Clark Bicentennial is creating the most significant intercultural dialogues in 200 years, according to Alan. "Tribal representatives serve on planning and advisory committees for events and exhibits, working hand in hand with people from other backgrounds," he says. "They're all sharing stories and traditions and gaining an appreciation for each other's cultures. I love the humor and wisdom of the native people."

Pageantry on the Grasslands

Rain and high winds keep us grounded in Sioux City for a second day, and on the third day we still can't fly because of fog and scattered showers. We learn of a native powwow going on 120 miles away in Pickstown, South Dakota, so five of us and a dog squeeze into the small cab of the truck for a two-hour drive.

Jack, our canine companion, is wedged in the center of the front seat. Rolling along through the countryside, he gets a whiff of an interesting animal odor coming through the air vents. He jumps on Sue's lap, opens the side window by pushing on the electric button, and pushes his nose out into the breeze. "Who taught him that trick?" I ask. "He figured it out by himself," Sue replies.

The powwow is held on a ceremonial field behind Fort Randall Casino, which belongs to the Yankton Sioux. The haunting, insistent beat of native drums leads us to the crest of a ridge overlooking the grand spectacle. Below us we see a circle of motion, music and color,

This structure would win the prize for "Smallest FBO Office. A chair and telephone provide the basics at Eagle Butte, South Dakota, while Mary and Sue wait on clearing weather.

MOBRIDGE, SOUTH DAKOTA

Lake Oahe, named from the Oahe Indian Mission established among the Lakota Sioux in 1874, borders the rolling hills of the prairie.
Over 230 miles long, the lake runs from Pierre, South Dakota, to near Bismarck, North Dakota.

The triangular Fort Mandan came to a point at the rear, where a sentry walked a catwalk each night through the bitter winter of 1804-1805. Lewis recorded temperatures sometimes as low as 45 degrees below zero, and on the coldest nights each sentry was on duty for no more than 15 to 30 minutes. Two rows of small rooms include a blacksmith shop, guardroom, interpreters' quarters, and six rooms for sleeping quarters.

set against golden grasslands stretching to the horizon. Yankton, Cheyenne River, Rosebud, and Santee Sioux are represented, along with the Omaha, Crow Creek, Ponca, and Lower Brule tribes. People aged 4 to 80 take their turns in dances that are sometimes elegantly restrained, sometimes lively and skillful, always a blaze of color. Young mothers sit in the stands holding babies in cradleboards. Four young girls take a fancy to Jack. They take him for a walk every 10 minutes, and fill his stomach with bits of fry bread.

Combining pageantry, socializing, competitions and traditional ceremonies, the festivities have been going on all weekend, and each new session starts with a dazzling grand entry. The dancers are led into the circle by an eagle staff bearer and an honor guard bearing the U.S. flag and tribal flags. Native Americans have the highest volunteerism rate for military service of all ethnic groups in the United States, and at powwows each veteran is introduced and honored.

Visitors are welcome here, but we're asked not to film parts of the ceremony that include sacred rituals of the tribes. People are happy to tell us the meaning of the traditional dances and chants. The stories stem from legends, from the preparation of warriors for hunting or battle, from celebrations of their success when they returned. The Grass Dance originated with a practical purpose: dancing feet flattened the tall grasses to prepare the field for a ceremony. In the Switch Dance, men and boys dress up as girls and women, and vice versa, each performing the traditional dance steps of the opposite sex. The crowd loves it, and prizes are given to the best performers.

The powwow takes place with a lot of friendly cheering, laughter and good sportsmanship, and with no haste. It's quite a cultural treat for us.

Orville Wright Coming In!

On the morning after our late night out, the air is hazy but calm, and we move on. Flying upstream along the Missouri, the land slowly and continually rises in elevation. We're climbing steadily upward above the back of a huge tortoise, the gently rounded curve of the continent's great interior.

From the air, we see uneven shorelines instead of the concrete channels and dams of the lower river. The portion of the river between Sioux City, Iowa, and Yankton, South Dakota, is one of the most natural stretches left on the Missouri. It's like the river Lewis and Clark knew, shallow with a wide floodplain. People love to canoe this stretch, where the braided streams flow in curves around islands and sandbars.

Concrete reappears near Yankton, where we overfly the first of several large dams that change the character of the Missouri through parts of South Dakota,

B I S M A R C K , N O R T H D A K O T A

Like spilled blue paint, the Missouri rolls across nearly level land. Near Bismarck the turquoise color of the Missouri contrasts strongly with the chocolate-brown waters near Kansas City.

Emanuel (Manny) Red Bear dons a ceremonial headdress.

Mary gives Ryan a lesson on her dulcimer, while Sue and Jack provide an audience.

North Dakota and Montana. Water management is controversial here, with the needs of a dwindling base of barge traffic being weighed against the need to restore natural habitat on the river.

After landing to take a break at Chamberlain, I join the ground crew for a while. We stay in touch with Ron by radio and communicate between the two RVs with walkie-talkies as we approach the High Plains town of Eagle Butte, on the Cheyenne River Sioux reservation.

Near here Lewis and Clark met the Teton Sioux, the "dwellers of the Prairie," who were known as fierce warriors. President Jefferson especially wanted to establish friendly relations with this tribe, which controlled trade along an extensive portion of the river. During three days of councils and celebrations, misunderstandings between the Captains and the natives almost led to violence twice. Though the Corps made no solid trade or peace agreements with the tribe, they at least won safe passage through the territory. Descendants of the Teton Sioux are now referred to by their traditional name, Lakota, meaning "friend" or "ally."

A Lakota friend of mine, Emanuel (Manny) Red Bear, is waiting to meet us at the airport. Ron makes a low pass to check the windsock. "It's Orville Wright coming in!" Manny declares, and Ron has acquired a nickname that will stick for a long time.

WATFORD CITY, NORTH DAKOTA

Like multicolored melted candles, an isolated area of badlands stands near Theodore Roosevelt State Park.

With Lakota Friends

Manny teaches the Lakota language and traditions at the local high school and community college, and he is committed to helping young people build strength and character in these difficult modern times. He's the great-great-grandson of Sitting Bull, the spiritual leader who inspired his people at the Battle of the Little Big Horn, the last major victory for the Plains Indians. Manny leads modern-day battles now as the tribe struggles to keep its culture alive.

Manny will travel to the Little Big Horn in Montana tomorrow to help dedicate a new national memorial to Sitting Bull. Two of Manny's cousins are at his house helping with the preparations. Ira Blue Coat, a descendant of the warrior Crazy Horse, has a wise-cracking sense of humor. He aspires to a position on the tribal council, and we predict he'll do well. Doug Peterson has taught in China as a Fulbright scholar, and now he teaches history at the high school on the reservation. Doug invites us to camp tonight at his ranch, and we are quickly set at ease in this extended family. Tom Van Norman, the tribe's attorney and state representative, joins us for dinner. Our talk turns to the history, current issues and future plans of the Lakota.

Before the waves of white settlement and the Indian wars, the Lakota Sioux and other Plains Indian tribes had a livelihood and society centered on the huge herds of buffalo that so amazed Lewis and Clark. By the early 1900s the buffalo had nearly been exterminated, and the U.S. government forced the Indians onto reservations. Native holdings were further reduced each time parts of their lands were wanted for settlement, railroads and mining.

Today, average incomes on the reservation are low, the social fabric is torn, and unemployment is high. Still, the Lakota are determined to find new pathways to prosperity while rebuilding spiritual and cultural traditions. Instead of building casinos to create jobs and revenue, as many tribes across the country have done in recent years, the Cheyenne River Lakota are looking for economic alternatives. They'll soon open a processing plant for buffalo meat and beef, and they are developing selected types of tourism focused on their wide-open spaces, fisheries, buffalo, elk and cattle herds, and a wild mustang protection program. Visiting the reservation, city dwellers like us can step back in time and reconnect with the natural world.

Rick Waters from the Triple U Ranch

Bouncing for Buffalo

Over the next few days we plan to stage our own buffalo hunt—with a camera. At first the weather is threatening, with low clouds and intermittent rain. We park the RVs at the airport at Eagle Butte and put up the satellite dish. Quickly checking online with the National Weather Service, we learn that the skies will clear soon. The Internet connection we take for granted at home has become a vital lifeline for us on the trip, especially in areas with no cell phone service.

We take off and glide over the rolling High Plains where kettle ponds are rimmed with dark green reeds. It's a short hop to Pierre, a small city centered around a graceful state capitol building.

On landing, Ron keeps our speed just slightly below cruise as we descend on a steep glideslope. He pulls power just as we flare over the runway, hoping no correction on the throttle is needed because a slight boost of thrust from those powerful engines could easily send us ballooning upwards. Controlling the plane during the landing roll takes some careful footwork, since the rudder is large and it's easy to over-correct any drift.

The quick responsiveness of the throttle can be lifesaving. Once a deer started to cross the runway as we were landing. A light touch on the throttle allowed us to climb rapidly, miss the animal and avoid disaster. A typical single-engine plane is just not as responsive as *Cloud Chaser*. "In my Cessna, that would have been impossible," Ron says.

At the airport in Pierre we ask where we can get some close-up photos of buffalo and find we've come to the right place. We head out in the truck for the Triple U Ranch. Much of the film *Dances With Wolves* was shot on location at this ranch, and it's one of Pierre's important tourist attractions.

Rick Waters greets us. He's a solid-built young man in a white cowboy hat. "We're here to take pictures of your buffalo," says Ron, "and the best light is right about now." Rick and his father are cooking buffalo steaks, but they hurriedly take them off the grill and we all pile into Rick's white Ford pickup, little suspecting that this is going to be the ride of a lifetime.

For two hours Rick pushes his truck to the limit, a little grin playing at the corners of his strawberry-blond moustache. We bounce up hillsides so steep that we're

PIERRE, SOUTH DAKOTA

Half-ton buffalo speckle the rolling prairie like coarsely ground pepper.

We found intricate Native American bead work in the Valley County Pioneer Museum in Glasgow, Montana.

sure we'll slide backwards any second. We drive in and out of deep draws and through swampy marshes, bumping our heads on the ceiling of the cab. The dog bounces around like a Ping-Pong ball until he wisely hunkers down on the floor. Finally we spot some buffalo on a hill ahead.

These are the ultimate free-range animals. They're purebred buffalo, *Bison bison bison* in redundant scientific jargon, with no domestic cattle genes. Rick does not vaccinate them, and their food is strictly prairie grass. They are hardy and well-suited to the high ranges. During a bad blizzard one year, Rick went out to check on his livestock. "Many of the cows were frozen dead. I dreaded seeing the buffalo, but when I got to them they were all still standing, heads into the wind—hadn't lost a single one."

Quietly and carefully, Ron gets out of the truck to attempt a photo. He's looking at 1,500-pound beasts that have a strange, almost human quality in their shapes and faces. It's something about the set of their eyes and the width of their noses. Cattle all seem to have the same vacant look, but on these majestic creatures every face is different. Every time Ron moves a step closer to the buffalo, they move away by three steps. This dance goes on for a while until Ron concludes that the only way to photograph the skittish giants will be from the air.

At dawn the next morning, we fly back to the Triple U. The grassy hills are sharply backlit as the sun comes up. The banks of Lake Oahe create graceful curves, with no trees—just prairie. The buffalo herd is magnificent from the air. Big bulls stroll imperiously, wearing robes of fur across their shoulders, and the calves walk at a cautious distance from the adults. Buffalo roll in the paths, stirring up huge dust clouds in the dry air. We fly low over the herd. This time the animals stay in place and Ron gets the picture he has in mind.

Heading toward the town of Mobridge we see no trees and flying low is easy. Cresting a ridge, we're suddenly over a prairie-dog town that looks like the surface of the moon—pockmarked with the holes of hundreds of Lewis' "barking squirrels." The prairie dogs are upright on their back legs, but they're camera shy. They pop down their holes faster than Ron can take their photo. I don't know who is more surprised, Ron or the rodents.

Prairie dogs on alert.

We descend again to the banks of the Missouri at Mobridge. In the evening tornado and flood watches are broadcast for nearby areas. Heavy rains pound our metal roofs like hammers on kettledrums, and high winds make the campers rock and shudder most of the night. Remembering that mobile homes seem to attract tornadoes, none of us get much sleep.

From Bismarck to Fort Mandan

The stormy skies clear slowly through the morning hours. In the afternoon we can make a straight shot north to Bismarck, North Dakota. En route, Ron reminisces about the first time he flew *Cloud Chaser*, right after he finished building the plane.

"I sat at the end of the runway for what seemed like forever," he says. "Images of those bags of rivets and cleco pins, sheet metal and the bare skeleton of the plane sitting in the hanger just a few months before kept running through my head. As the engines hummed behind me, I kept wondering if this thing was airworthy—will it fly?"

"But," he continues, "I swallowed hard and rolled onto the runway, pushed the throttle full forward. As I took off, all I could

Jack goes door-to-door, conducting a census of prairie-dog burrows.

see in front of me was sky, and all I could feel was my stomach dropping, roller coaster-style. I looked down off my right side and now the runway looked like a sidewalk. In 30 seconds I was at 1,500 feet, already out of the traffic pattern before I got halfway down the runway."

The sun lights up the grasses on the "empty" prairie, highlighting a rich mixture of grasses for the buffalo.

Most planes cover a lot more asphalt before they lumber into the sky, and they're a considerable distance away from the numbered edge of the runway by the time they get to cruising altitude. "It's like taking off in a fighter jet," he says, and I laugh at the comparison. "I also have a fantasy of landing on an aircraft carrier with no arresting device. *Cloud Chaser* could do it too," Ron says.

At Bismarck the airport is busy and local reporters turn out to cover our story. The airport lineman escorts the media to the runway to get footage of our flight demonstration. Ryan mans the back seat of the plane. As he and Ron are poised for take-off he urges, "Come on Dad, let's show 'em what we've got!"

Ron suspects that the cameraman will miss the shot the first time because he'll focus on a liftoff point much further down the field. Ron makes several passes with

Cloud Chaser so the cameraman can get his shot. We are always amazed at the intense excitement the plane engenders.

All 55,000 residents of this crisp and neat city seem to have Bicentennial fever. The Corps of Discovery spent the winter of 1804-1805 just north of town at the Mandan Villages, and area residents are proud of it. Bismarck is planning a Lewis and Clark event that will include a "Pitchfork Fondue" party. Each person will select a huge beefsteak, spear it with a pitchfork and have it cooked over an open fire.

Exploring the town, we discover that North Dakota has tutored everyone from tourism professionals to retail sales clerks on Lewis and Clark history. Gas station attendants, taxi drivers and anyone else who greets visitors can speak on the subject. This enormous educational campaign is reaching thousands of families. On any test of 1800s history, North Dakotans would spoil the curve for the rest of us.

Ron and I are up before dawn in the morning, again bartering sleep for adventure and leaving a quiet campground where no one else is stirring. At 5:30 a.m. the Bismarck tower has just opened, and our small green *Cloud Chaser* is the only plane moving. The controller tells us to use "any runway, your choice, any intersection." Climbing to 11,000 feet for a photo, we can almost touch the scattered remnants of last night's storm clouds.

At the town of Washburn we fly over Fort Mandan, the replica of the Corps' home for the bitterly cold winter. The Captains chose the location because it was near the Knife River villages of the Mandan and Hidatsa tribes, a community that had between 3,000 and 5,000 residents, more than St. Louis or Washington, DC, at the time. The Indians welcomed the explorers and helped them survive. Chief Big White of the Mandans told Captain Clark, "If we eat, you Shall eat, if we Starve, you must Starve also." Through the long winter, the Corps traded with their Indian neighbors and shared evenings of entertainment with them.

In April 1805 the Corps sent the keelboat back to St. Louis with a small crew carrying copies of the Captains' journals, plant and animal specimens they had collected in the first year of the journey, and "sundery articles to be sent to the President of the United States."

Leaving Fort Mandan, Lewis, Clark and 29 men launched the pirogues and the huge dugout canoes they had made from cottonwood trees during the winter. With the interpreter Charbonneau, his wife, Sacagawea, and their infant son, they set out to

KILLDEER, NORTH DAKOTA

Glowing in the distance, this large yellow canola field looks like it could be a caution sign, signaling danger ahead.

The imposing towers of Fort Peck Dam dominate a gigantic spillway. This dam is one of the largest earth-filled river impediments in the world.

travel about 1,500 miles to the west into regions that were uncharted and full of new challenges.

Floodplains and Farms

Between Bismarck and Pickstown we glide over the only free-flowing section of the Missouri River in North Dakota. The banks are lined with remnants of the rich floodplain forests Lewis and Clark saw, where piping plovers, least terns and fall-migrating whooping cranes still use the sandbars in the river. In the farmland beyond, a huge field has haystacks scattered around like checkers on a giant game board.

Above a major dam at Pickstown is Lake Sacagawea, an expanse of water so wide that it has the feel of an inland sea. On our map the lake looks like an aneurism, a long bulge in the thin line of the Missouri.

New Town is the headquarters of the Three Affiliated Tribes, comprised of descendants of the Mandan, Hidatsa and Arikara people who were once numerous in the region. The rebirth of spring and summer in North Dakota paints the landscape. Huge canary-yellow blocks of color in the abstract canvas below us are canola fields in full bloom, and a field of blue flax smells like lavender. As we land for a quick rest stop, a meadowlark serenades us at the edge of the runway, its song rippling like the laughter of children.

At the airport local people tell us that family farming in America is rapidly changing. High capital costs and unpredictability of income are driving young people toward other occupations. Contractors plant and harvest crops on multiple farms on a "cash rental" basis, supplying the equipment needed and guaranteeing fixed revenues to the landowners. The gorgeous farmlands we've been seeing are crucial to the global economy's future, since the world will need to double its food production in the next 50 years to accommodate population growth.

In the afternoon the ride gets bumpy as we encounter "thermals." The ground reflects the sun's heat unevenly, and thermals are the result—columns of warm air rising sharply above the patches of ground that are warmest. *Cloud Chaser* rides a windy elevator up and down for nearly an hour before we land at Watford City.

We camp nearby at Theodore Roosevelt National Park, in a territory so remote and little known that only a handful of tourists visit each year. This national treasure is a diamond in the rough. Buffalo, antelope, deer, bighorn sheep and feral horses inhabit the preserve. The next morning we soar over the eerie badlands of the park and its environs—forbidding country that was dubbed "bad lands to cross" by early frontiersmen. The cliffs and rock formations are a study in the weirdly beautiful, the phantasmagorical.

WOLF POINT, MONTANA
Here in the tranquil farmlands of eastern Montana the Missouri seems to pause in contemplation. Not until it reaches Sioux City will the river act like it's late for an appointment with the sea.

BISMARCK, NORTH DAKOTA

Peering down through the clouds from 12,000 feet, the landscape looks like wrinkled green velvet.

LAKE OAHE, SOUTH DAKOTA
The undulating span of this bridge mimics the shape of the hills on the horizon.

YANKTON, SOUTH DAKOTA
In addition to spinning water into gold, the Gavins Point Dam provides recreation and flood protection.
Many dams along the Missouri spark controversy because of the changes they bring to the river.

Stands of trees make a butterfly-like pattern among the manicured farms along the Missouri.

CHAPTER FOUR

Flying the Missouri Breaks

Pelicans float beside us in the sky, unthreatened by our aerial presence. With their bright white feathers, these birds can be seen from many miles away, huddled in small groups along the river. They were a tremendous curiosity to the Lewis and Clark crew.

GETTING TO THE MISSOURI RIVER BREAKS, A canyon in nearly roadless country, is not easy by any mode of travel. The nearest public airport we could use as a base of operations is a hundred miles away. To be over the river in time to shoot photos at first light, we'd have to fly in the dark over empty terrain for hours—not a good option.

We land at Glasgow, Montana, to plan our strategy. Local folks give Ron the phone number of Clyde Robinson, a rancher located just 10 miles from the Breaks. Clyde has no objection to visitors dropping in out of the sky, so he gives Ron the latitude and longitude coordinates for his grass strip in the middle of Montana's open country.

I'm with the ground crew today, and Clyde has directed us to "drive south, turn onto a dirt road beside eight hay bales and go two more miles." We could be in the savannahs of Africa—for 50 miles we see no buildings, billboards or even telephone poles, just a beautiful treeless plain, with yellow sweet clover and blue-gray sage at the roadside.

Ron arrives at the ranch before we do. He circles for landing, but the "grass strip" has no grass! It's just bare dirt with ridges, bumps, two slopes and a dogleg at the end. He touches down and bumps along, sounding like a hammer being dragged across a corrugated metal roof. As Ron settles in a cloud of dust, Clyde asks, "How did you like my strip? I just built it yesterday, and you're the first to try it."

Resting in a pasture in the middle of Montana, Cloud Chaser, *like the Mars lander, probably feels the urge to transmit its findings back to Earth. Sue and Jack survey a place for our campsite.*

MISSOURI BREAKS, MONTANA

*Nature's artistry is revealed when the low morning light bounces between the
white canyon walls to display colors revealed by the eons of erosion.*

On a brisk June morning I depart from Glasgow, Montana, and point the flying green canoe south to rejoin the Missouri River. For the first leg of today's very long trip, I decide to stay at 1,500 feet. This higher altitude lets me study the general lay of the land. Below me lie endless miles of vast, eroded landscape. From this height I can barely make out small herds of antelope on the run. In the distance the river pops into view then looms ever larger. Now I resume the path of my watery highway westward.

After another hour of flying, the exotic walls of the river canyon start teasing me to put my camera into action. As I slowly circle an interesting land formation, a composition starts to develop in my mind. The only problem is that a turbulent thermal is swirling upwards at the exact viewpoint where I need to shoot. I set my camera shutter speed high enough— hopefully—to handle whatever the thermal can dish out. Bracing for what lies ahead, *Cloud Chaser* and I dive into the invisible wall of turbulence, shoot a couple of frames and then exit to an area of relative calm. Unsure whether I was really able to

Eroded cliffs in the Missouri Breaks.

freeze the action, I dive back in for another round, then another. It's like riding a Brahma bull at a rodeo, or at least a slightly irritated Holstein cow. Unlike a rodeo though, the only audience and prize for me will come months later if the photos are successful.

As I fly ever westward, the terrain looks even more foreboding. The river winds to the north and then to the south. With every mile the rugged ridges and peaks take on a less airplane-friendly look. On my Global Positioning System (GPS) moving map display I have marked a lonely little destination waypoint in the middle of Montana: a grass strip on an isolated 70,000-acre ranch where I've made arrangements to land. I recall that my flight-

training manual said I should design a flight plan that takes me to my destination airport in a way that avoids hostile terrain. But here I am alone, in hostile terrain, and with not a single airport within a hundred miles. My twin engines really are my security blanket now.

After another hour and a half, I'm smack dab in the middle of the Missouri Breaks, due south of the ranch. It is now the middle of the day, and this kind of lighting just won't do for photos. I decide to spend another hour in the air scouting for shots that I'll do during twilight. I set several GPS waypoints according to the camera angles I will want, using round markers for morning shots, triangles for evening shots and square ones for views that could work either way.

Feeling satisfied that I have scouted at least 60 miles in either direction of the ranch, I climb to about 1,000 feet over the top of the mesa and adjust my heading for my grass-strip destination. Finally the ranch is in sight, and I notice a couple of humans below—the first ones I've seen in four hours. I circle the field to check the windsock and make a low approach. The runway has two major humps in it. No time for the eenie-meanie routine. By instinct, I pick the second hump to let my wheels touch down and roll out on rough but solid ground.

The ranch owner and his daughter greet me warmly. They seem as surprised as I am that I arrived alive in this thing. After studying the aircraft for a few minutes, trying to figure out whether it most resembles a canoe, a grasshopper, a praying mantis or a pterodactyl, my hosts ask the usual questions about the construction and specifications. I explain that, no, the green *Cloud Chaser* is not made by John Deere. It's a unique machine that has brought me to meet new friends in the big-sky country of Montana.

MISSOURI BREAKS, MONTANA

Like an artery of life, the Missouri turns the land green wherever it touches.

Three generations of Robinsons live and work on the ranch, in love with a lifestyle that seems a bit lonely to us. But the children are lively and hearty, having learned hunting and ranching first-hand. They travel 45 miles to the nearest high school, sometimes living in town during the winter months.

To escape the lowland heat, we camp in Zortman, a cool hideaway just 10 miles from the ranch. The town is nestled in the Little Rocky Mountains, an isolated cluster of peaks that stands in strange relief some 3,000 feet above the surrounding plains. The slopes are deeply forested with aspen, birch and ponderosa pine. Gold nuggets and ore valued at about $25 million have been mined near here off and on since the 1890s. This is definitely an off time, and the local economy is at low ebb. Zortman is glad to see a few wandering travelers like ourselves.

Leading the way to Clyde Robinson's ranch, antelope race effortlessly across the valley floor. These animals often seem to run just for the pure fun of it. People sometimes hunt them here, but antelope meat has a powerful gamey flavor from a diet heavy in sage.

(right) Practically hovering over the Missouri Breaks, we float above a drab gray canyon 2,000 feet below. As the sun creeps over the horizon, the whole canyon gradually comes alive with color.

A Linear Wonderland

At four a.m. Clyde Robinson's ranch animals are still asleep as *Cloud Chaser* climbs effortlessly into fresh cold air. In the delicate light of dawn, the rolling rangeland is a soft skin on the earth, dimpled and creased like a baby's knees. I watch the surface of the earth as if it might move at any moment, the muscles gently flexing beneath it.

We intend to stay aloft as long as the morning light holds. "Are you cold?" Ron asks. "Chilled to the bone," I answer, "but it's ok." The slipstream air on my cheeks feels like it's blowing out of a deep freeze, but it doesn't matter. This morning we are en route to photograph the crown jewels of the Missouri River.

NEAR FT. BENTON, MONTANA

A blue ribbon of water brings calmness to the otherwise chaotic landscape.

MISSOURI BREAKS, MONTANA

Suddenly from behind a rock formation a herd of bighorn sheep emerges out of the shadows. While Mary takes control of Cloud Chaser,
I quickly switch to a telephoto lens. As we drift by, barely above stall speed, the herd gathers on a grassy ledge and I snap their group portrait.

In 20 minutes we arrive at a wild and rugged canyon that's ominous in the dim light. Jagged cliffs reach upward toward us, forming the "broken country" for which the Missouri River Breaks are named. We arrive just as the eastern horizon begins to brighten.

In a museum in Glasgow, we're fascinated to find a belt buckle, photos, and news clippings about a 20th century Assiniboine leader who earned the name "Chief First-to-Fly" by daring to ride in an airplane.

Below us the spectacular sandstone cliffs start to glow. The rocks come awake at the touch of the sun and burst into fiery orange before our eyes. In a heartbeat the river flashes from gray to turquoise.

"Who rode that into town?" passing locals might wonder. Tied to a hitching post in front of the Zortman jail, Jack waits patiently while the crew eats at the local diner.

The air is so smooth that it takes only the lightest touch on the controls to turn, swoop or climb at will. As we follow each new turn of the river, the display of carved rock ledges changes endlessly. We float over a linear wonderland with minarets, knife-edge pinnacles, mushroom-capped pillars and the sheer vertical White Cliffs that captivated Lewis and Clark.

In the side canyons, smaller streams are trying to imitate what the Missouri has done. Across narrow gorges, the stacked ledges look like apartment buildings facing each other across city streets, so close that neighbors could talk to each other from upstairs windows. But this is a village without gossip or politics, inhabited only by cliff swallows.

The scene has hardly been touched since Lewis and Clark's day. No roads run parallel to the canyon, and only two bridges cross its 149-mile length, each joining some dirt roads and a lonely cabin or two. The only humans we see in two hours of flying are a few rafters on a float trip. In 1976 the U.S. Congress designated this remote stretch a National Wild and Scenic River, and in 2001 President Clinton named the area surrounding it the Upper Missouri River Breaks National Monument.

In this dramatic setting the Captains decided to honor two women who waited back east. Clark named the Judith River for Julia Judith Hancock, who would become his bride two years after his return. Lewis named the Marias River, whose banks were "garnished with one continued garden of roses," for his cousin Maria Wood.

Flying back to the ranch, the sun has warmed the land, and we are on a wildlife safari. From the air we can see shy backcountry creatures that would never show themselves near

MISSOURI BREAKS, MONTANA
Millions of flowers cover a mesa like a dusting of yellow snow.

Morning comes very early in Montana in July. We arise at 4 a.m. to the sound of coyotes on the distant hills. While Sue prepares an abbreviated breakfast, Mary and I prep the plane and release it from its tie downs. In the very early twilight Jack spots an antelope near the RV. Even though Jack instantly makes it to full throttle, the antelope doesn't even bother to go beyond first gear.

While Mary dons her helmet and goggles and climbs to her perch behind me and beneath the wing , I start the engines by flipping the master switch to "on," mags "on," primers "on."

I trip the toggle to fire up the right engine. High-compression ROTAX engines require a lot of energy to move the piston inside the cylinder wall—a more violent explosion occurs than with a lower compression engine—so you're dealing with a bigger firecracker. They're more temperamental to start, but the extra horsepower they give is worth it. The engine catches, quickly settling down to a quiet purr. I watch the oil temperature gauge slowly climb to 120 degrees, warm enough for take off.

We taxi to the end of the strip. To my left the flashing light of my wing strobes illuminates Ryan and Sue holding Jack. The dog might chase the plane, but as yet we have never seen him actually lift off. Set for short-field takeoff to minimize contact with the rough ground, we accelerate rapidly. Within seconds we are climbing far above the ranch and turning south to the Missouri.

My course heading is set for my most-favored waypoint. Within 15 minutes we are circling over the dimly lit canyon. Below us the river winds gracefully through the gorge. The smoothness of the river contrasts strongly with the fractal cliff walls of the canyon. The plane is now trimmed for level slow flight and the camera ready for action.

As the sun starts creeping into view, my anxiety starts to build to a fever pitch. It might seem that my priority thoughts are keeping the plane in the air and getting the right camera setting. But that's not the case! After over 750 hours flying my kit-built plane and 40 years using a camera, both tools feel like extensions of my body that I use almost instinctively. The only anxiety I feel has to do with the creative process. The fear of seeing a beautiful scene and not being able to express it to others in a powerful and unique

Near Fort Benton.

composition is tormenting. I fear not being able to cover enough ground in the small amount of time before losing that wonderful light. If only this thing had an afterburner.

Now the yellow glow of the rising sun starts to kiss the tops of the rugged land below. The cool blue color of the morning sky illuminates the remainder of the scene. After shooting several shots, I apply the throttle to climb another 1,000 feet and repeat the process. Within seconds new views unfold. To hold my position in the sky, I resort to pivoting on my wing tip, banking to the left and then to the right, or diving an ear-popping 2,000 feet per minute—whatever it takes to get a variety of shots in the least amount of time. At the rate we are changing altitude and darting around, a fisherman on the river below might think he is seeing half a dogfight. As soon as I feel satisfied about the shots, I raise the flaps and zip over to another ridge where the light is starting to bring out hidden details.

The whole process is repeated for the next 20 miles up river. Even though I have my spare, and highly qualified, pilot in the back seat chomping at the bit, I can't turn over control of the plane until I am through shooting—letting someone else fly would interrupt the intuitive process. When the light and textures are changing as fast as the fleeting expression on a child's face, it allows me no time to give out directional instructions to another pilot.

Looking down on the landscape in this part of the country, I think about how different my perspective of the land is compared to that of Lewis and Clark. As they traveled the river by boat, they saw greenery all around them and probably wondered whether this lushness extended far beyond their viewpoint. But from my elevated perspective, I can see how quickly the land turns to brown and nearly unusable arid landscape just a short distance from the river. Suspended high above the terrain here in central Montana, the Missouri resembles a giant life-giving artery that provides nourishment through out the Northwest.

After this incredible flight, we point *Cloud Chaser* back toward the ranch. Having been in the air nearly three hours now, our hunger triggers thoughts of an incredible meal of juicy antelope or elk steak, but knowing Sue and Ryan's limited hunting skills with weaponry, the thought quickly fades.

roads. Ron's telephoto lens catches 20 light brown animals on a rock ledge beneath the top of the canyon wall. They are bighorn sheep, and their forebears were plentiful 200 years ago in this region.

It's time for a hot breakfast, and at our campsite Sue and Ryan have made omelets and strong coffee with chicory. Nothing has ever tasted better. We recount our flight at length, savoring every detail. This is one we'll remember forever.

Time-Warp Town and Fractal Landscapes

Taking to the air again en route to Great Falls, we overfly Fort Benton, a pretty little town that retains 1800s style. It sits on a flat shelf along a curve of the river and was once the terminus for steamships traveling upstream on the Missouri.

Along the next stretch of the river, a giant artist has carved the cliffs into a fractal landscape. We talk about the cleverness of nature using fractal patterns to build branching trees, snowflakes and crystals—repeating a single geometric form thousands of times to make a shape that looks like itself at all different magnifications.

Here rain and snow erode the small channels, and the small channels merge to cut larger channels that have the same form. Something about this geometry is captivating in a primal way. It's beautiful both visually and mathematically. Artists and mathematicians create fractals on their own, but they can't match the originals we see below us.

It's hard to imagine that today's flight can be topped, but we've got spectacular country ahead. In camp we review the route we will take to what Lewis described as "...the grandest site I ever beheld...," a waterfall of "...perfect white foam which assumes a thousand forms in a moment...," the Great Falls of the Missouri.

At this spot, known as Decision point, the captains were unsure which fork was the Missouri. Splitting up into two parties, they explored both routes. The southern leg (bottom left) turned out to be the continuation of the Missouri River.

MISSOURI BREAKS, MONTANA

Resembling a moat running beside a castle wall, the Missouri reinforces a virtually impenetrable barrier towards the south.

WHITE CLIFFS, MONTANA

On our morning tour through the nature museum, we discover a new gallery room filled with abstract white monoliths,
probably a collection from a creator's cubist period.

MISSOURI BREAKS, MONTANA

Leaving the mountain and canyon adventure behind, the Missouri River heads eastward for the calmness of flatter land.

NEAR FORT BENTON, MONTANA
Colorful fields of barley accent the fractal-patterned badlands.

NEAR FT. BENTON, MONTANA

This shallow river canyon only whets the appetite of adventurous boaters for what lies ahead.

WHITE CLIFFS AREA, MONTANA
Erosion seems to bring these rocks almost to life in this formation resembling a bear's foot.

MISSOURI BREAKS, MONTANA
Like a sliver of blue sky that fell to the canyon floor, the smooth Missouri contrasts with its harsh surroundings.

WHITE CLIFFS, MONTANA
The orderly ways of man complement the chaos of nature.

CHAPTER FIVE

Threshold of the Rockies

ON JUNE 13, 1805, CAPTAIN LEWIS AND A SMALL SCOUTING PARTY HEARD
"... A roaring too tremendious to be mistaken for any cause short of the great falls of
the Missouri." They saw "spray arise above the plain like a column of smoke." Lewis
wished he were an accomplished artist or poet
"... that I might be enabled to give to the
enlightened world some just idea of this truly
magnificent and sublimely grand object, which
has from the commencement of time been
concealed from the view of civilized man...."

Our own first glimpse of the Great Falls of
the Missouri is just a tease. At 2,500 feet, we're too
high above them to get a good photo, and if we
descend, the gusty winds below us would toss
Cloud Chaser around like a toy. All we want to do
is to find the airport, brave the turbulence for as
long as it takes to land, and get on the ground. In
the strong headwind, we use only 20 feet of the
3,000-foot runway to land, and turning the plane
into the crosswind to taxi to the ramp takes a bit of
muscle. Aerial photography will have to wait for a
better day.

For many years the falls have borne little
resemblance to the five cataracts that Lewis
described. Over the past century, they have been
forcibly altered and their thunderous roar has been
dulled. In the early 1900s, dams were built at the
top of four of the falls for power production. Lakes

*Frozen in time, the captains stand looking westward. This sculpture also honors York,
William Clark's slave and manservant who made the long journey with the expedition.
York was the first African American many of the Indians had seen, and he became a
popular figure among them. York asked for his freedom after the journey, and it seems
that Clark granted the request several years later.*

GREAT FALLS, MONTANA
Though the falls are now stifled by a tranquil lake and dam, their roar still seems to echo between the canyon walls.

Near the Interpretive Center is Giant Springs, one of the largest freshwater springs in the world. Clark described this wonder as "... the largest fountain or Spring I ever Saw, and doubt if it is not the largest in America Known, this water boils up from under...rocks near the edge of the river... ." A flow of more than six million gallons per day emerges from cracks in the sandstone and washes over ledges on the shore of the Missouri.

have formed behind the dams, and one of the falls is totally submerged. The region gained electricity but lost a national treasure.

Although the falls have been tamed, the adventures of the Corps of Discovery are well-remembered here. The excellent Lewis and Clark Interpretive Center has made the town of Great Falls a sort of capital of the Bicentennial. At the Center we get a true sense of the grueling portage Lewis and Clark made to bypass the giant waterfalls.

Standing at the base of a two-story display, we look up at lifesize mannequins of men in buckskins and moccasins. Struggling for footing on jagged rocks, they are moving a massive canoe up a steep hillside, pushing from the sides of the boat and pulling it with ropes from the top of a cliff, every muscle straining. The dugout is a hollowed-out trunk of an enormous cottonwood tree, and it's canted at a horrifically steep angle. Underfoot, the spiny cacti pierce the men's moccasins. The sun is blistering hot, jaws are clenched. By power of muscle and power of will, the Corps is determined to succeed.

A Hidatsa chief at the Knife River villages had told the Captains of a tremendous waterfall ahead, and they expected to find a single cataract that they could go around in a day. Instead, they confronted five falls and a series of rapids along nearly twenty miles of the river. The first waterfall was 97 feet high, and all of the falls formed insurmountable barriers to navigation. The backbreaking portage took nearly a month.

Lewis and Clark encamped just upstream of the falls after their ordeal, and here they celebrated the Fourth of July holiday in 1805. Entertaining themselves with singing and dancing, the Corps finished off the last of their supply of "spirits." We're fortunate to be in town to commemorate Independence Day nearly 200 years later.

Great Falls provides ample entertainment for visitors now. A parade shows off the local Lewis and Clark Honor Guard, as well as marching bands, cowboys and horses in their finest regalia, and anything motorized. All vintages of fire engines, tractors and even racing lawnmowers show up for this small-town, homespun event in the heartland of America.

In the late evening, spectacular fireworks announce themselves with thundering reports. Rocket trails of color shoot upward and burst high above the Missouri River. In the water, reflected spheres of light rise from the depths and split into parallel bars, pulsing outward to make an aurora borealis at our feet. The celebration dissolves the boundaries between air, water, city and people. On the Fourth of July, every town in America is everyone's hometown—we wouldn't be strangers anywhere.

FORT BENTON, MONTANA

In its heyday 50 steamboats a season docked at the levee here, bringing supplies and equipment and loading gold to be shipped back to St. Louis. As ranchers and farmers occupied the plains, Fort Benton became a hub for trade and travel.

The Gates of the Mountains confront us after weeks of flying over vast open plains and prairies.
The progressively more confining space of these huge granite walls brings a growing sense of uneasiness.

Photographer's Notes: **Missouri River Romance**

Studying all the maps and aerial photos of the Missouri River I thought I knew its every nuance. It never occurred to me that all the hours I would spend admiring her beauty from the air would lead to more than a casual relationship. Perhaps I am spending too much time in the cockpit, but this river came to seem increasingly like a sensuous woman to me.

The two years researching her geography did little more than keep our first encounter from feeling like a blind date. Now I'm spending most of my waking hours either capturing her best features with photos or negotiating the difficult air currents that occasionally come between us or planning the next flight to survey her charms.

The lower 800 miles of her length were smooth and tan, flowing in gradual curves like shapely legs. The oxbows showed evidence that she had exercised her prerogative to change direction. Rising gradually to the high plains of the Dakotas and east Montana, she took on more depth and character. Near Glasgow, Montana, the river turned turquoise and very clear, as if she was revealing her soul.

At the Missouri Breaks the erosion of the steep canyon walls said that this lady has experience. At last, reaching the headwaters at Three Forks, the delicately curling streams of the Gallatin, Madison and Jefferson Rivers flowed like the waves in her hair.

For six weeks and thousands of miles I have studied her every curve and tributary. Sometimes I ascended thousands of feet into the sky just to see more of her at one time. Other times I dipped so low as to nearly touch her rippling surface and smell the cottonwoods on her sandy shores. Often I climbed into the cockpit before dawn so I could see—and photograph—her shining first expression in the morning glow.

In this evolving intimacy, I came to appreciate not just her spectacular beauty but the subtleties of her everyday self.

Flying over her headwaters now, I wonder if she will be upset when I leave to cross the Rockies and visit the Clearwater, Snake and Columbia Rivers. Blowing the Missouri a kiss, *Cloud Chaser* and I begin our ascent over the mountains.

THREE FORKS, MONTANA

Like two silvery serpents, the Jefferson and Madison Rivers inch their way across the valley floor. Another mile further they will become entwined with the Gallatin to form the mighty Missouri River.

JEFFERSON RIVER AT THREE FORKS, MONTANA

Now far from its snowflake birth in the distant mountains, the Jefferson River is about to shed its youth at the headwaters of the Missouri.

Shooting the Falls

In the morning the winds still won't give us ideal conditions for flight, but we're eager to push on, and we take to the air. As always, Ron has studied his options for routes, altitudes and positioning using 3-D maps and satellite imagery, so he's done the best possible planning to get the shots he wants. Last winter, using the computer, he "flew" the whole route from his comfortable chair, but now the true test is at hand. In the real world of winds, other air traffic and changeable lighting, he counts down a string of photographer's mental worry beads, considering the choices he'll make to produce the best picture.

Whenever Ron is flying and doing photography, he's using several sets of skills. As he approaches his subject area, he slows the plane by decreasing throttle and deploying flaps. He positions the airplane on a heading that allows him to cruise past the subject in a gentle arc and then maintains that heading by using his feet on the rudder pedals. When flying solo and doing this, he relies on a well-honed sense of the "attitude" or three dimensional orientation of the airplane. Although his hands are on the camera and he's looking through the viewfinder, he can sense any change in the orientation of the airplane and quickly bring a hand back to the control stick to correct it.

Over the Great Falls, Ron decides that he wants the dam to be part of the composition. He chooses angles that show how the concrete structure slides in behind the stair-step falls, adding to the original rock ledges, with the creased and folded landscape as backdrop. Against the rough textures of the tall riverbanks, the stream has cut a channel like a clean incision.

Gates of the Mountains

Leaving the Great Falls area, we have a panoramic overview of the city. The small Sun River enters the Missouri from the west, and the Missouri bends to embrace downtown Great Falls on three sides. This town has put its rivers at center stage with a winding parkway and bike trail that run beside the Missouri for 10 miles, letting people get close to the water.

We look for the place Lewis and Clark called the "gates of the mountains," where the Missouri cut a narrow canyon through an isolated range that presages the dense Rocky Mountains beyond. We are moving into a new realm where the character of the landscape changes abruptly—the High Plains region gives way to a world of numerous separate ranges interspersed with broad open valleys in southwest Montana.

Continually looking for new angles, lighting and photographic techniques to bring an artistic image out of the unedited world passing before him, Ron feels excited and just a bit nervous about the beautiful and sometimes treacherous terrain we'll be crossing. He knows the combination of flying and photography will challenge *Cloud Chaser*'s ability— and his own.

Between the towns of Cascade and Wolf Creek, the Adel Mountains loom wine-dark over a gorgeous canyon of the Missouri. The rocks below us are of a rare volcanic type called shonkinite, darker than basalt and glinting with black crystals. The other-worldly black crags trigger a sort of primal fear. This could be the dramatic formation Lewis and Clark called the "gates of the mountains," but scholars have debated the issue.

We cross another valley and arrive above the second location that might be the site the explorers described. This canyon is the one now advertised as the Gates of the Mountains. It's a magnificent three-mile gap cut through light-colored rock. Near-vertical limestone cliffs tower 1,200 feet above the river.

Beyond Helena, the small capital city of Montana, we follow the Missouri to the town of Three Forks. Here the high ranges of the Rockies make a stunning appearance on the far horizon. The sight of the jagged high peaks brings to mind the challenges of mountain flying that lie ahead.

We land and park *Cloud Chaser* against the backdrop of the enormous peaks we want to cross in a few days. Somehow the little craft looks smaller and more fragile than it did when we set out this morning. Captain Lewis expressed our sentiments exactly in his journal: "While I viewed these mountains I felt a secret pleasure in finding myself so near the head of the heretofore conceived boundless Missouri; but when I reflected on the difficulties which this snowey barrier would most probably throw in my way to the Pacific... it in some measure counterballanced the joy I had felt...but as I have always held it a crime to anticipate evils I will believe it a good comfortable road untill I am compelled to beleive differently."

Curlicue Streams

The town of Three Forks has a sub-alpine feel. Broad valleys lie between lofty ranges still tinged with snow in July. The three small streams that descend from the heights to join here have historically been world-class trout streams. Although one of them now suffers from low flows due to withdrawals for agriculture, the other two remain deep and cold enough to provide excellent sport fishing. In the spring, when snowmelt fills them to the brim, they're ideal for float trips.

On our morning photography flight, we laugh at the antics of the streams—they've drawn crazy curlicues all over the level surface of this broad valley. They turn and twist repeatedly in circuitous routes, making little forward progress per mile traversed. The ground is marked with thousands of remnants of their previous wanderings, shallow half-circles and arcs impressed into the rich loam of the meadows.

Lewis and Clark named the three forks the Jefferson, Madison and Gallatin Rivers in honor of great Americans who were critical players in the purchase of the Louisiana Territory: President Thomas Jefferson, his close friend and advisor James Madison, and Secretary of the Treasury Albert Gallatin. The confluence of the three streams is sometimes

The next leg of the trip, we choose to follow the Madison River, flying parallel along the Madison Range towards West Yellowstone, Montana. The topo maps show the mountains gradually rising to 10,000 feet with the only break a mile-wide canyon pass at Quake Lake. Training and experience tell me that midday heating will probably turn that pass into a natural wind tunnel. I need to slip through the pass before the winds pick up.

Leaving Ennis-Big Sky Airport before dawn, I head toward the town of Ennis and the river valley I scouted the day before. The ride, for some reason, is not as smooth as I thought it would be. There's nothing like starting the day off shooting photos while being jerked around by turbulence.

Heading south along the river, I figure because of my detour to shoot photos, I'm now "chasing my chase crew" as well as Lewis and Clark. Another hour into the flight, I spot them on the highway ahead. Swooping down near the flat valley floor I'm now running parallel to our truck and RV. Jack is the first to notice me, then Ryan and Sue wave excitedly at my sudden appearance.

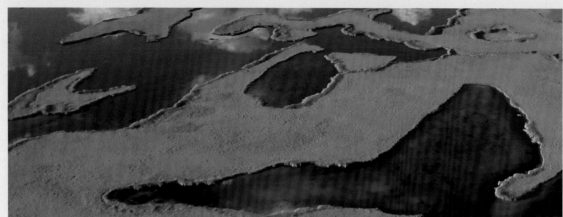

Abstract textures in the marsh at Swan Lake.

I return to cruising altitude and speed as the canyon at Quake Lake begins to loom into view. Cautiously approaching the deep canyon, I try to sample the wind currents. Unaccustomed to flying around these high peaks, I'm a little nervous. Since everything seems OK, I decide to go for it. Flying above the lake, I see the awesome remnants of the earthquake's devastation. Calculating that the winds are only 10 mph with light turbulence, I make a few circular passes to explore and shoot photos. With some relief, I exit the pass after a few minutes and proceed to the airport.

The FBO at West Yellowstone advises me about wind direction and speed, the active runway and the firefighting cargo plane in the traffic pattern. Wary about wake turbulence from the huge plane, I give it plenty of time to get on the ground. With the airport elevation at 6,600 feet, the high altitude coupled with high temperatures can be a tricky situation for most non-turbo powered aircraft. *Cloud Chaser,* on the other hand, has no problem. It typically lands and takes off in less than 200 feet. Even with the high altitude of the airport boosting that distance to 600 feet, I have an extra 8,000 feet of runway to play with.

As I tie down the plane, several pilots and aircraft mechanics come over to check it out. When I land my other plane, a 1978 Cessna 172, the typical comment is "nice paint job." *Cloud Chaser* always seems to draw a crowd from out of nowhere to study every facet of its style, performance and construction.

We camp near Yellowstone Park. After recovering from sticker shock of the campground cost and thinking the high prices must be related to the altitude, we drive over to check out Quake Lake and arrive at the visitors center about 3 p.m., the wind feels like it is trying to rip the door off as we exit the truck. No doubt now that we made the right decision to get through the pass early.

Waking the next day to the sound of distant coyotes yelping, Sue and I head off to the airport to prep the plane. In the chill of predawn darkness we instinctively bundle up for what will probably be at least a two-and-a-half hour flight. After takeoff we head west toward Henry's Lake at about 1,000 feet. The mountains are starting to brighten with the morning glow of twilight. To our left the Centennial Mountains run like a picket fence along the southernmost edge of Montana. I think to myself, *If I can't do great things with such incredible scenery, I must surely be flawed.*

As we start our climb that will put us in the upper valley at Red Rock Lake, the air temperature starts to rise noticeably, and sudden violent turbulence interrupts our peaceful ride. Looking down to see how much the trees are blowing beneath us, I'm surprised to see no movement in the branches. Since the sun hasn't had a chance to heat the valley floor, the turbulence must mean we're at the edge of inversion layers (warm air sitting on top of cold air). I decide to climb above it. Wow, what a difference! During the 1,000-foot climb, the temperature went from 38 to 79 degrees Fahrenheit. Sue and I are definitely feeling overdressed now. In east Tennessee I seldom see more than a 15-degree difference.

A lake so large and smooth that it appears like a mirage on the horizon lies in front of us. The textures of the clouds repeat flawlessly on the water. Usually it is a struggle to sort out the elements to arrive at a powerful composition, but here it's too easy. It seems like a potential artistic masterpiece stretches out before us in every direction.

UPPER RED ROCK LAKE, MONTANA

The mirror-like surface of Red Rock Lake appears to have been placed there to give a double dose of beauty to this hidden paradise.

In 1959 a violent earthquake in the Madison River area triggered a massive landslide. Tons of earth and rock slid down the sides of mountains with catastrophic results. The landslide brought the river to an abrupt halt, damming it in this canyon and creating Earthquake Lake or Quake Lake, a 190-foot deep lake.

called the headwaters of the Missouri. From this point downstream the river officially takes that name, but geographers designate another spot on a tributary of the Jefferson River as the actual source of the Missouri.

Lewis and Clark ascended the Jefferson River and then its largest branch, the Beaverhead River. From Camp Fortunate, a place now inundated by Clark Canyon Reservoir, Lewis followed Horse Prairie Creek, a tributary of the Beaverhead River. He mistakenly thought the creek was the headwaters of the Missouri, and he wrote that one of the privates, Hugh McNeal, "... exultantly stood with a foot on each side of this little rivulet and thanked his god that he had lived to bestride the mighty & heretofore deemed endless Missouri."

Another tributary of the Beaverhead, the Red Rock River, would have taken Lewis to the place about a hundred miles away that geographers now designate as the ultimate headwaters. The furthest point from which waters flow into the Missouri is at a small tributary of the Red Rock Lakes near Yellowstone National Park. We leave the Corps' route to find the lakes, now the home of a remote national wildlife refuge nestled in mountains near the juncture of Montana, Wyoming and Idaho.

We follow the valley of the Madison River upstream as it rises to the Ennis-Big Sky Airport at 5,400 feet. This place is an outpost of paradise, isolated and beautiful. Camping next to the airport, we have the majestic Madison Range behind us and the valley floor at our front door. We love to stay near a small airport, living almost alongside *Cloud Chaser*, now and then hearing the sound of another plane landing. Tonight we sit outside and watch a brilliant sunset.

After a stop at Yellowstone, we are ready to make an attempt at two mountain passes that lead to the Red Rock Lakes. *Cloud Chaser* rides the bumpy edge of an extreme thermal inversion—warm air is trapping cold air below, and the edges of the two layers are ragged where they meet. Our discomfort is rewarded with a magnificent view. The remote shallow lakes, the pristine source waters of the muddy Missouri we have traveled for a month, are sparkling mirrors in the clear morning light.

ENNIS, MONTANA
The long and undulating oasis of the Madison River brings life-giving water to trees that spring up along the banks.

ENNIS, MONTANA

Dwarfed by mountains of the Madison Range, Cloud Chaser *and crew reunite at Ennis Big-Sky airport.*

We knew the same supplies the Corps of Discovery carried on their expedition weren't going to work for our trip because the FAA frowns on carrying weapons, black powder and whiskey onboard an aircraft. It turns out that our most important cargo was a Visa card, cell phone and bug spray. We did think, halfway through our trip, that a shotgun would have been better for those pesky, large mosquitoes.

While the Corps of Discovery had to deal with strong river currents and undertows, we dealt with air currents such as wind shear, thermals, inversion layers and mountain downdrafts.

Their friendly encounters with the Native Americans helped them get horses and supplies. The friendships we made provided us places to land the plane, camp and take photographs.

When Lewis and Clark made their journey, they were equipped with the most technologically advanced tools of their era. No one had better rifles and navigational equipment than they did. To Lewis and Clark, the term "shooting" meant survival. To us "shooting" was only done with a camera to preserve our visual experiences. No animals or native Americans were harmed during the making of this book. We were equipped with the best tools as well. For centuries adventurers have depended on a compass, but to us it was simply a backup tool. Instead, we had an armada of GPS satellites floating above the earth pinpointing our every move. Using GPS as the main navigation tool, I could compute destination, present position, directional bearing, ground speed, altitude, estimated time of arrival and many other facts about our flight.

Equipped with a DataStorm™ satellite dish on the RV, we had a broadband connection to the Internet, enabling us to send email and upload images to our web site from even the most remote area.

Weather is the single most important factor related to flying. For Lewis and Clark, trudging through a storm was no big deal. But bad weather is something that must be avoided with aircraft, especially ours. Using the internet enabled us to get instant reports about winds and storm forecasts. In the near future, we will be able to get weather information right in the cockpit as we are flying.

Cell phones and walkie-talkies were our other communication tools. We were really surprised at the good cell coverage we had in almost every location. The walkie-talkies let us coordinate between vehicles. Using a computer workstation and laptop, we downloaded and edited images from digital cameras, create web pages, distribute press releases and study all sorts of maps. These kinds of conveniences would have been impossible just a few years ago.

3D map imagery from Delorme

A replica of Clark's compass (far left) contrasts with our GPS, WAC chart and other piloting tools (above). We used 3D topographical maps (left) as well as satellite imagery for planning the best places for photography.

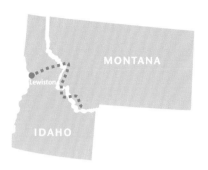

CHAPTER SIX

Challenge of the Mountains

WE HEAD NORTHWEST TO REJOIN LEWIS AND CLARK'S ROUTE ALONG THE Beaverhead River near the town of Dillon. A landmark for our approach to the airfield is Beaverhead Rock, a distinctive limestone hill standing alone on the plateau. When Sacagawea recognized the rock, she knew the Corps was near the Shoshone homeland she had left as a child.

Looking at an oversized aviation map on the Dillon airport office wall, we're a bit stunned to see the various ranges of the Rockies that we must cross, shown in an expanded scale. The greatest aviation challenges of our trip await us. Here Lewis and Clark were at a critical point in their journey as well. They were in desperate need of horses to help them cross the mountains before winter set in. Clark took the main body of the Corps to the forks of the Beaverhead River a few miles south

Ron preflights the plane before taking off.

of here and camped at a spot now inundated by Clark Canyon Reservoir. Lewis took a small scouting party ahead hoping to find the Indians, obtain horses and determine the best way to traverse the mountains.

Lewis eventually made contact with Shoshone leaders and invited them to meet at the camp Clark had established in the valley below. When Chief Cameahwait sat in council with the Captains, he met Sacagawea and discovered she was his long-lost sister. The event was joyous for all. The Shoshone provided horses and information, and the Captains appropriately named the site Camp Fortunate.

After caching the canoes at the camp to await their return, the Corps traveled on foot, with the horses carrying supplies. They set out to cross the Continental Divide at Lemhi Pass. Since the Divide was the western boundary of the newly purchased Louisiana Territory, they would soon be entering foreign-claimed lands.

Lewis and Clark had little knowledge of the Rockies, which appeared as only a single range on the speculative maps of their day.

A red barn at the foothills of the Rockies glows in the early morning sun.

BITTERROOT MOUNTAINS, MONTANA

This may only be a 10,000-foot mountain to the locals, but I see it as my "Mt. Everest" for the day.

Lewis wrote that Sacagawea identified, "This hill she says her nation calls the Beaver's Head, from a conceived resemblance of it's figure to the head of that animal." It was a welcome landmark.

When they set out from St. Louis, they expected to pass through the "Shining Mountains," as they were called at the time, in just two or three days and then make a moderate descent to the plains of the Columbia River.

Although the Captains may have gotten a clearer idea of the challenges ahead as they questioned native people along the way, many writers speculate about what was in Lewis' mind as he stood at Lemhi Pass with a small advance party, looking at the Rockies for the first time. Lewis merely wrote that he saw ahead the "...immence ranges of high mountains still to the West of us with their tops partially covered with snow." Ultimately, the crossing took more than two months on foot and horseback, and the explorers put to rest forever the age-old dream of a Northwest Passage as a practicable water and portage route to the Pacific Ocean.

At our campground in Dillon we study the terrain ahead and plan our own crossing of the Great Divide. Satellite imagery shows chaotic ranges of mountains with scattered high valleys ahead. Although we plot a route that will minimize our time over rocky terrain with nowhere to land, we must cross some daunting stretches. Ron and I have mountain-flying experience in other regions of the country, but the prospect before us is still sobering. Crossing the Rockies, by whatever means, is a metaphor for challenge.

It's a sleepy Sunday morning downtown in the frontier town of Hamilton.

BITTERROOT VALLEY, MONTANA

In the haze of evening light the Bitterroot Mountains resemble a creased curtain that separates Montana from Idaho.

BITTERROOT RIVER VALLEY, MONTANA
Anglers wave to us as they drift by at the mercy of nature's transit system.

Across the Divide

The morning dawns fair and calm for our flight over the tallest mountains we'll face on our entire journey. It's time to depart, and for a brief moment I ask myself why I thought I wanted to do this. "Let's review plans A, B and C one more time," I suggest. We study the aviation charts again for the shortest routes to safety should something go wrong. We talk about how we'll test the air continually for downdrafts or mountain waves that could be dangerous and always be ready to beat a retreat. "Let's do it," says Ron, and I'm ready.

Southwest along the Beaverhead River, the land rises gradually and *Cloud Chaser* climbs confidently toward Lemhi Pass—a rounded saddle at 7,300 feet between tree-lined ridges. As we come over the top, the rugged folds of the pass give way to the rows of jagged peaks that Lewis saw. Heading north, the landscape becomes even more rugged.

Like a sea of white-tipped stony waves, the ranges to our right and left seem to spread out forever. Their granite crests form the long, curving backbone of the continent, where the world's foundation is pushed high into the air. Our engines hum steadily in the icy air as we climb toward the Great Divide, the defining line where the rivers run to the east on one side and to the west on the other. A trumpet call in my head seems to announce the opening of a new world.

We've done it, crossed the Continental Divide in a flying machine not much bigger than a canoe, with the wind in our faces and some of the nation's most rugged mountains not far below our feet. For a while we float outside of time. We follow a fork

(above) In the late evening light, a deer slowly emerges from its shelter of pines.
(right) Sue, Ryan and Jack take a break to wade in a cool mountain stream.

With a slight glow of the approaching dawn in the sky, we depart Dillon, Montana, on a perfectly calm and beautiful morning. Banking the plane to point the nose directly at those snow-capped mountains to the west, I begin my gradual ascent. When I spied those distant peaks three days ago, my anxiety started to build. Now's the day of reckoning. For the past two days we have been studying topo maps, weather forecasts and, of course, Lewis and Clark's journals. Knowing that our route today calls for crossing two high mountain passes, I packed the rear cargo area with containers of extra fuel, camping gear and food in case the weather changes and we have to set down in a field for the night.

Comparing the topo map to the journals, I couldn't help but wonder at their crisscrossing route through those rugged mountains into Idaho on their way to the Pacific. Of course I wouldn't have seen so much of this incredible country if they had taken a shorter way.

As I make my way up the eastern slope of the Beaver Head Mountains, the sunlight livens up the textures on the mountainside. Below me a small herd of elk wanders through a meadow. Now floating above Lemhi Pass, I lower my speed to swing in a graceful circle to relish the view. To the east, Montana is bathing in sunshine. Over to the west, Idaho's Lemhi Valley is still deep in shadow.

Prospectors used to scour these mountains for rare gems and gold veins, chipping away with blistered hands at rocks that showed promise but yielded nothing. In my hunt for photos, I can relate. But I guess the only blister I could incur would be on the tip of my forefinger from snapping the shutter.

Sometimes I fly for hours or days over beautiful landscapes in what I call scouting mode. Then the magic happens, and everything comes together—like finding a hidden gem—to make a unique and powerful composition. If the lighting, textures and colors don't work together, though, it's just another colorful scene.

Interesting how when one prospector hits the mother lode, all the others head for the same area to look for "the daughter." This wonderful country of ours has a lot of beautiful parks, and each one of them attracts artists and photographers like a magnet. That's good,

The Selway River snakes through a canyon in the Clearwater Mountains.

because it leaves the rest of the country for me! Beauty is everywhere, but finding the gems takes work. The most rewarding compliment I get is when people say they have been living somewhere all their life but never realized the place's beauty until they saw my photograph.

As we descend into the Lemhi Valley, I scout around for possible camera angles until the sun makes its appearance. I would love to land and explore the valley, but I'd lose the morning light in the process. After 20 minutes of slow flight, the shadows rapidly retreat to the east. Exposed before me is a lush green valley floor nourished by the Salmon River. Surrounded by steep brown mountains on three sides, it reminds me of a "lost world" movie I saw as a kid, except there are no dinosaurs roaming the valley below.

We head north and begin our climb over the Lost Trail Pass and make a slow circle to absorb one last view. Now after conquering my second and last mountain pass for the morning, I am feeling more confident.

As I close in on our destination of Hamilton in the Bitterroot Valley, the temptation of those snow-capped giants is too much. Experiencing some of the mountain climber's "because they are there" syndrome, I apply the throttle and climb to 11,000 feet. The landscape before me is so immense I feel like I am not moving and the world has stopped spinning.

The calm air relaxes me, but looking at the jagged peaks below and beside me, I fully comprehend the fragility of my aircraft. Knowing that the fabric on my wings is no thicker than the skin on my body makes me uneasy. To the locals these are just 10,000-foot mountains, but they are my "Mt. Everest" for the day.

We descend to the valley to defrost our faces. Although my mind has been vastly nourished by the experience of the four-and-a-half-hour flight, the growl of my stomach is competing with the sound of the engines. Wishing we could have stayed longer, we land at Hamilton, Montana. We're far ahead of the chase crew who had to take a much longer route by highway, so we use the airport courtesy car to race away to the nearest eatery.

Lewis and Clark struggled for days to cross these mountain passes, we took only hours, a commercial jet takes minutes and the Space Shuttle the blink of an eye.

LEMHI VALLEY, IDAHO

Retreating shadows of the morning sun unveil a study in contrasts. Runoff flowing to the south has inscribed its converging network pattern twice, gouging deep canyons in the brown hills, while faintly scoring the green valley with tiny streams that merge to form the Salmon River.

LEMHI PASS, MONTANA

Accentuated by the glancing blow of morning light, a nearby mountain resembles the molting fur on a buffalo's back.

of the Salmon River, which the Captains named the "River of No Return," then re-cross the Continental Divide twice at Lost Trail Pass. Slipping through the pass we congratulate ourselves. We've passed over the steep rooftop of the earth two times in one day. Descending the north side of Lost Trail Pass we pick up the Bitterroot River and follow it down into its spectacular valley.

At Hamilton's airport, midway up the valley, a dozen private and corporate jets crowd the flightline as they await well-heeled fishermen and timber industry executives. Parked beside the sleek white jets, the lightweight *Cloud Chaser* is a bird of a different feather, one that has carried us across the Great Divide in a manner that the high-flyers could not imagine. Our little craft draws a crowd, seemingly from nowhere. Later some reporters appear, eager to see our unique plane and hear about our adventure—and we never tire of telling our story.

In Search of Moose

Ron announces that he wants to photograph a moose. He makes a trip into town to get advice from knowledgeable locals. "Take a ride up Lost Horse Canyon in the Bitterroot Range," they say. Either they didn't tell him, or he didn't tell us, that we'd rumble over a rock-strewn and gullied dirt road that would pitch us against the walls of the truck cab and rattle our bones for 18 miles.

We ascend to the jewel-like Twin Lakes perched amid granite outcrops of the massive Idaho Batholith, the core of the magnificent Bitterroot Range. We find a picnic area and a corral with two horses high in this canyon but no moose, at least not this evening. Still, we can wander small ravines carpeted with alpine wildflowers—yellow shooting stars, penstemon and showy mounds of beargrass with pungent white flower heads. We wait at the edge of a lake as the sun begins to slip behind the peaks. On the opposite shore two coppery deer emerge from the forest for a last drink, and Ron frames a

A giant of the forest, this bull elk takes notice of our passing.

telephoto shot. The next day Ron finds his moose—in front of a modern hotel, grazing in a pond just 25 feet off the highway at Lolo Hot Springs.

At the north end of the Bitterroot Valley Lewis and Clark camped near Lolo Creek, which they called "Travellers rest." They followed the creek upstream to Lolo Hot Springs, where Clark found the water to be "... nearly boiling hot at the places it Spouted from the rocks... ." Continuing westward, the Corps began a 10 day passage across the Bitterroot Range. It was probably the most difficult part of their entire journey. They climbed to Lolo Pass and hoped to follow the Lochsa River downstream but found that the riverbanks were impassibly narrow and obstructed with fallen logs. They were forced to begin an arduous trek on a Nez Perce trail along the crest of the range.

The Corps struggled through hail and snow in the high country in early September. Finding no game, the company became weakened from lack of food. On the Lolo Trail, the Corps' campsites now bear witness to their ordeal, including Hungery Creek, Portable Soup Camp, Jerusalem Artichokes Camp and Horse Steak Meadow, where in desperation they killed and ate one of their horses.

In the morning we fly the route of the explorers' grueling trek across the Bitterroot Range in a couple of hours. The ride is comfortable, but we're alert every moment. *Cloud Chaser* can land on any reasonably flat patch of earth 200 feet long, if necessary, but over the Lolo Trail few such options are available to us. We cross Lolo Pass safely and trace a route along the Lochsa River, another rocky, unnavigable and breathtaking stream. This is the first in a stair-step sequence of streams that eventually led Lewis and Clark to the Pacific Ocean. Deep green and dense forests of western red cedar are below us. The tall straight trees are slim arrows pointing toward the sky.

LOLO PASS, MONTANA
Blue has given way to yellow now in a hidden meadow flush in a tapestry of flowers.

Yellow butterweed rings an open glade in timbered country near Lolo Pass. Earlier in summer the high flat ground is filled with the blue flowers of camas plants. Camas or "quamash" roots were a staple food that the Indians shared with the Corps when the half-starved company descended from the snows of the Bitterroot Range on their outbound journey. In the spring of 1806 during the return trip, Lewis described camas at the peak of its color: "...From the colour of its bloom at a short distance it resembles lakes of fine clear water, so complete is this deseption that on first sight I could have swoarn it was water."

LOST TRAIL PASS, MONTANA

Though this was the most treacherous and challenging pass for the Corps, thanks to the kind winds, it was only a mildly bumpy ride for us.

CHAPTER SEVEN

Descent Into the Unknown

OUR AERIAL ROUTE TAKES US ACROSS THE NARROW NECK OF NORTH CENTRAL Idaho where the state is only 100 miles wide. It's a spectacular region. At the hamlet of Lowell, the Lochsa and Selway Rivers join to form the Middle Fork of the Clearwater River. Huge boulders have toppled from the cliffs into the stream, and the evergreen forest is cool, dark and fragrant. Just a few miles further to the west, we leave the rich national forests and tumbling mountain streams behind, and fly over a world of treeless but fertile plains cut by river gorges.

Here the Corps of Discovery at last descended from the cold Bitterroot Range to lands known only to the natives. Enormously relieved to reach the prairie at present-day Weippe, Idaho, Lewis wrote, "... The pleasure I now felt in having tryumphed over the rocky Mountains and decending once more to a level and fertile country where there was every rational hope of finding a comfortable subsistence for myself and party can be more readily conceived than expressed, nor was the flattering prospect of the final success of the expedition less pleasing."

The company was welcomed by the Nez Perce Indians, whose lodges dotted the meadows during the fall harvest of wild camas roots. The natives shared meals of roots and dried fish with the half-starved explorers and gave them information about the route ahead. Clark described the Nez Perce as "... Stout likely men, handsom women, and verry dressey in their way, the dress of the men are a white Buffalow robe or Elk Skin dressed with Beeds....The women dress in a Shirt of Ibex, or <goat> Skins... ornamented with quilled Brass...Beeds, Shells & curios bones...."

The Corps crossed the prairie to the Clearwater River. They were gaining some strength after their ordeal in the

Ron inspects the engines before a photo flight.

Circling to land at Kamiah, I notice one of those "Paul Bunyan toothpick factories" below me.

WALLA WALLA, WASHINGTON
A green puddle of cultivated field in a foreboding landscape proves once again that man can tame the wilds of planet Earth.

With a forecast of moderate winds, I depart at the crack of dawn from Hermiston, Oregon, thinking that I would be able to reach Portland before the winds could build and flex their muscle. It didn't take long to realize that the westerly winds had been tipped off that I am coming. Starting with a ground speed of 70 mph that rapidly decayed to 40, I decided to climb another 2,000 feet. No good either—the ground speed dropped another 10 mph, and the turbulence was just as bad.

An hour into the flight, the landmarks below have barely changed. The ground speed is now at 25 mph and the turbulence is like holding the business end of Zorro's whip. I figured out in a hurry that this was not a fun day to fly.

I notify my chase crew by radio, "I'm heading for the municipal airport at Arlington." I reference my GPS for the airport coordinates. Banking back to the southeast, a strong rear quartering tail wind gets me to the airport quickly. Circling the field to check the windsock, it doesn't take me long to figure out which terminal is for domestic and which is for international arrivals and departures.

Normally I try to target the numbers at the threshold of the runway for my landing. As it turns out, there are no numbers, no threshold, not even a runway. The barely defined landing strip begins as grass then transitions to dirt and gravel.

Although this landscape is monochomatic, these bizarre brown textures are captivating.

After touchdown I look around at a deserted airport. Above the tall weeds in the distance are a few broken-down shacks and one possible usable hangar. I hear the sound of an engine in an old shed beside the hangar and I walk over to investigate. In the dim window light amidst the clutter of engine parts is a really big guy kneeling down with his back to me. He's adjusting the carburetor on a running lawnmower. When I approach and tap him on the shoulder, he drops his screwdriver, throws his arms in the air and begs me not to kill him.

After regaining our lost composure—mine from laughter and his from fear—we become friends. With the wind now howling, he helps me anchor the plane on the protected side of the hanger.

When the chase crew reaches Arlington they stop in a small café and ask for directions to the airport. "What airport?" the locals respond, unaware that they even have an airstrip. After meeting half the town, the crew gets directions and make their way up the dusty road to the top of the mesa and meet me. We set up camp then take a break and head for the local park by the river to swim.

By sunset, the wind dies down, and we sit in lawn chairs beside the plane and RVs to watch the stars and listen to the coyotes in the distance. As the sky darkens, the veils of the Milky Way begin to appear and the night sky puts on a spectacular show.

LEWISTON, IDAHO

Inching along to its final destination at Lewiston, the paddlewheeler Queen of the West *looks like a toy against the vast wall of rock.*

Approaching from over a mesa, the Orofino runway looks like a leftover straight piece of highway that couldn't be bent around the mountain.

mountains, but the Captains and nearly all the men were sick from their unfamiliar diet. They found excellent timber a few miles downstream from present day Orofino and encamped at that spot for two weeks to build canoes for the run to the ocean. The Nez Perce showed them an efficient method of burning the pulp of the tree trunks to make it easier to carve out. Chiefs Twisted Hair and Tetoharsky agreed to accompany the travelers to guide them and to smooth their way with other native bands.

A Split-Level World

The airport at Orofino sits on a narrow bench of land beside the Clearwater River at the bottom of a slot canyon, on a level spot just wide enough for a single runway. Descending between two mountainsides, our aerial view encompasses both parts of a split-level world.

The river canyon cuts through the sunny plateau like a dark serrated knife. At the base of the cut, a world of small towns exists along the shaded stream, surrounded by timbered canyon walls. No one in the valley can see that there's a second world 2,000 feet above. On top of the canyon walls, miles of golden grassland farms are spread across the tableland.

In the morning we make a short flight along the Clearwater River to its confluence with the Snake River at the twin cities of Lewiston, Idaho, and Clarkston, Washington. When Lewis and Clark reached this place, they found only a single Indian cabin. The namesake cities that now face each other across the Snake are busy transportation and industrial centers. We're still above a split-level world. We land at the Lewiston airport on the high ground some 700 feet above the cities.

Waiting for our ground crew, Ron and I sit outside on a bench at the ramp. A local couple are prepping their small Cessna for flight, and we can't help overhearing their

Ethyl Green proudly shows off one of the Nez Perce Appaloosa horses.

LEWISTON, IDAHO

With help from the glow of the setting sun, I pull a "Rumplestiltskin" and turn hay rolls to gold.

Nestled in the valley at the confluence of the Snake and Clearwater Rivers, Lewiston and Clarkston compete for historical importance.

conversation. The woman takes a look at *Cloud Chaser* and asks her husband, "What kind of plane is that green one?" "Oh, that's just an ultralight," he answers. "They're fun, but they can't go very far." Having flown 6,500 miles already on this trip, Ron mutters under his breath, "Yeah, an ultralight on steroids."

First Solo in the Green Canoe

At the dock in Clarkston is a colorful sternwheeler that has brought tourists upstream from Portland and points west. Sightseers transfer to small "jet boats" that take them on a day excursion into Hells Canyon, a twisting and rugged place also known as the Grand Canyon of the Snake River. The gorge at Hells Canyon cuts 5,500 feet below its walls in some places, and it's the deepest gorge in North America.

Ron wants to take some air-to-air photos of *Cloud Chaser* flying over the spectacular cliffs, and this is the chance I've been waiting for. Much to Ron's dismay, he can't fly his beautiful airplane and be aloft in another plane to take its picture at the same time. He'll have to rent a second plane as a photography platform, and I'll get to make my maiden solo flight in the green dragonfly.

Weighing in at 115 pounds, this lady pilot won't be heavy enough in the front seat to keep *Cloud Chaser*'s nose down properly. On the way to the airport, we buy some sand and a nylon sack with a drawstring top. Thirty pounds of weight on the floorboard under my legs ought to do the trick.

I climb into the front seat, and for the first time in *Cloud Chaser*'s life, Ron takes the back seat. I'll do some maneuvers and several takeoffs and landings to get the feel of the plane while I have a pro with me. Sitting so far forward and close to the small stubbed nose of the plane, I feel I'm out on the very end of a limb, but I'm ready to give it a try.

On my first takeoff I bring the power up gingerly, and climb out at a shallow angle like I do in other airplanes I fly. "Just push that throttle full forward—it won't break," says a voice on the intercom. On landing Ron says to leave the flaps up. It will be a faster approach but less destabilizing. The plane swerves on touchdown, but I manhandle the rudders as I was instructed to do, and we roll out just fine.

LEWISTON, IDAHO

Like a small green bug, Cloud Chaser *descends into a canyon on the Snake River with Mary at the controls.*

I'm still processing all this when I need to talk to the tower, and my mouth won't work right. I can't quite get my tongue around "nine-four-four-romeo-lima requests taxi back for takeoff," and it comes out unintelligible. Laughter erupts over the intercom from the back seat.

After a few more landings, I can talk and fly at the same time, so I'm ready. Ron gets in a small Cessna with a local pilot, and I lead out in *Cloud Chaser* to get in position over a beautiful part of the canyon in time for the best evening light.

I reach the rendezvous point over a remote field far from any farmhouse when the late-evening sun is turning the wheat below to 24-carat gold. In half an hour this day will fade, never to return in precisely the same way again. Warmth radiates from the rich wheat itself, but no one else has come by land or by air to feel it. While I wait for the second plane, I circle slowly over the field, tracing its curved edges and cutting lazy figure-eights in the air, playing in the same soft breeze that ripples the grain below.

Flying alone has its own special rewards. The field of new grain perched on the edge of an ancient dark cliff is my confidant, and we share a quiet secret—the smell and feel of the air on this one irreplaceable evening. My engines hum softly. Suddenly the radio crackles and Ron says, "We have you in sight. Fly half a mile south, then make a 360 over the river at 4,500 feet while we come up beside you." The reverie is over, and I come alert to fly as precisely as I can, so Ron can capture the scene in the way he wants. It takes several passes, and we land just before dark, giving each other a high-five for our evening's work.

The Legendary Horsemen of the Nez Perce

We've planned our day around a visit to the Nez Perce Reservation, a short drive east from Lewiston. Native holdings were whittled away after the discovery of gold here in the 1860s, and the reservation is now one-tenth of its original size. At the tribal headquarters in Lapwai, we meet Ethyl Greene, who is coordinating Lewis and Clark activities for her tribe. Talking with her, we enter the world of legendary horsemen of the northwest.

The Nez Perce have lived in the valleys of the Clearwater and Snake Rivers and their tributaries for many thousands of years. They moved between summer and winter camps where they fished, hunted deer and elk, and gathered roots and berries. Early fur trappers gave them the name Nez Perce, or "pierced nose," though facial piercing was not a common practice among them. Tribe members prefer their own name for themselves, the Nimiipuu, meaning simply "the people." During the 1700s they became excellent horse riders and breeders. Captain Clark called the Nez Perce horses "... strong active and well formed. Those people have emence numbers of them 50 or 60 or a Hundred head is not unusial for an individual to possess."

The Nez Perce developed the forerunner of the modern Appaloosa horse. Ethyl tells us that the tribe is renewing its riding and horse breeding prowess. "We are developing the perfect horse," she explains, "by crossing the sturdy Appaloosas with an Asian desert breed

A lonely barn sits beside a lonely crooked road on a lonely mesa near Hells Canyon.

LEWISTON, IDAHO

The landscape of rolling ridges resembles melted chocolate accented with mint green.

The Clearwater River cuts a crooked path through the valley just outside of Lewiston. Chinook salmon and steelhead trout still fill the river, while elk, mule deer and mountain goats live in the nearby Selway-Bitterroot Wilderness area.

known for stamina, beauty and performance." The breeding program revives pride and tradition while it builds a profitable business, and the tribe's Young Horseman Program trains each new generation to continue the work.

From the Snake to the Columbia

Following the Snake River as it cuts diagonally across the southeastern corner of the state of Washington, we glide over four hydroelectric dams within a hundred mile stretch of river. At the sides of the dams are concrete "fish ladders" that salmon and steelhead must climb as they ascend the river to spawn. I spot some gravel landing strips at the river's edge near the dams. "Want to go fishing?" I ask Ron. If we had our tackle with us, we could land and try our luck.

At Pasco, the Snake spills into the mighty Columbia, the major river of the Northwest. Here the Columbia is on a southward course from its origins in Canada. After a short excursion to the east, the river will turn westward to meet the ocean some 328 river miles ahead, passing through one of most spectacular gorges in the world.

Sacagawea State Park and Interpretive Center is at the confluence of the Snake and the Columbia. A peaceful, shaded grove marks the point where Lewis and Clark arrived at the river. The park honors Sacagawea, the only female who made the journey with the Corps of Discovery.

Very little was written about Sacagawea in the journals of the Corps, and stories of her life after the expedition are controversial. The Captains did note her skill and courage. She often gathered wild plants that she knew would be important supplements to the company's wilderness diet, and in at least one instance she retrieved equipment and records that had fallen overboard when the canoes were nearly swamped. She carried her infant son across the continent, and her presence as a female member of the explorers' party assured many native tribes that the Corps did not have warlike intentions.

LEWISTON, IDAHO

Distant farm buildings sit in a valley of the most strangely contoured farmland we have yet encountered.

Rows of trees used as windbreaks on the farms appear as backlit feathers stuck in the ground.

Cropdusters and Cappuccino Fields

South of McNary Dam, watermelons and other crops are irrigated in circular fields that look like gigantic green tiddlywinks spread out on a playing board. We land at the Hermiston airport, home base for a rainbow assortment of brightly colored cropduster planes. We talk with the pilots and arrange to meet one of them for a 5:30 a.m. run to photograph him from above as he sprays the fields.

We arrive at the airport in the dark at 4:30 a.m. to untie the plane and fuel it for the flight. Like farmers and photographers, cropdusters begin work early. We are airborne before even the slightest glow in the east. Our plans are to coordinate positions with the ag pilot by radio, but we find we're on different frequencies. Luckily we've discussed GPS coordinates ahead of time with the pilot, so we know exactly where he will be spraying.

The sun is just beginning to warm the horizon. We make a quick detour to grab a picture of a barge heading upriver. Back on course, it's a short hop to the right crop circle. The cropduster pilot is delivering his spray precisely over the field, wasting nothing. Staying far above the ag pilot's working altitude, Ron flies a more irregular course, maneuvering relative to the sun to backlight the spray from the plane below us. We are mesmerized as we watch the bright yellow plane sweeping back and forth, making perfect passes across a circle of green.

On an evening flight, we skim over "strip-farmed" fields. Long bare strips that are currently left fallow to rest the soil are the color of mocha cappuccino. They alternate with stands of wheat that are honey-gold in the late light, making a repeating pattern on a grand scale —good for the land and beautiful too. We discover a wildlife haven near the river, a marshy refuge for deer, osprey, blue heron and white pelicans in this mostly arid land.

KAMIAH, IDAHO

*As the Clearwater River continues westward into Idaho, the land textures take on a dramatic new look. The endless
sea of tall pines gives way to an increasingly arid landscape.*

PLYMOUTH, WASHINGTON

Hundreds of irrigated circular fields dot the landscape like tiddlywinks scattered across the otherwise arid landscape.

Cropdusters, or "aerial application pilots," Gene Maahs and Ted Pasicka say the job is intense: they travel fast and low while identifying crop locations, controlling the spraying, and looking out for trees, posts and irrigation risers at the same time. "Sometimes we're flying at 140 mph just 10 feet over the ground," Ted tells us. "The hours are long, but we often run our own businesses, there's not much out-of-town travel, and we're at home every night."

Agricultural planes have to be rugged enough to perform as many as 100 takeoffs and landings in a day, ranging from asphalt airports to dirt strips in croplands. The pilots have to account for every drop, wasting nothing. In addition to spreading chemicals and fertilizer, they seed fields when they can apply it better or less expensively than ground equipment. Onboard computers coupled with GPS allow them to deliver and monitor their spray with exacting precision. Turbo engines have made agricultural spraying much safer and more reliable because there is less engine failure.

PLYMOUTH, WASHINGTON

With mathematical precision, this cropduster deposits its pixie dust on circular fields below.

LEWISTON, IDAHO

Through the illusionary magic of aerial perspective, a pulp mill's aeration pond resembles pastel blooms in a garden.

PASCO, WASHINGTON
Like a smudge on my canvas, a distant barge inches its way toward Pasco.

CHAPTER EIGHT

Columbia River Passage to the Sea

ANXIOUS TO SEE THE MAGNIFICENT COLUMBIA RIVER GORGE, WE TAKE OFF from Arlington. The white-topped peak of Mt. Hood appears on the horizon, standing incongruously 10,000 feet higher than the surrounding terrain. It's a vision that hints of dramatic scenes ahead.

Approaching the eastern end of the gorge, a region filled with unbelievable sights and rich history opens before us. Over thousands of years, native tribes came to terms with this rare environment and developed fishing and trading cultures on the river all the way to the coast.

Chinook mask of spruce with abalone eyes.

The strange beauty of the Columbia River Gorge is the result of one of the incredible dramas of the planet. Immense primal forces have created a deep and mysterious canyon that slices through dark rock. The rounded tops of the canyon walls are covered with short dry grass, but the exposed lava rocks form shelves and ledges where the river has cut through. We pass stacks of columnar basalt, squared-off columns arrayed like organ pipes. The cracked and jointed rock is the color of darkest sepia.

From telltale signs written in rock strata, and from soils and boulders that have traveled hundreds of miles from their sources, geologists have created a storyboard of gigantic events that occurred over millennia to create this landscape. Huge

Paddlewheeler and wind surfers compete for recreation on the river.

COLUMBIA RIVER GORGE WITH MT. HOOD AND MT. JEFFERSON

Like a single stitch in the landscape, the Bridge of the Gods links Washington to Oregon in this deep chasm of the Columbia Gorge.

A loaded barge chugs upstream through Swanson Canyon on the Columbia River.

eruptions of basalt lava occurred in northeastern Oregon at least 200 times over millions of years, covering 65,000 square miles.

The lava cooled into vast plates that hardened and collided, creating random folds in the new surface of the earth, but the Columbia River found a pathway through the folds of rock.

Much later, glaciers created ice dams that impounded the Clark Fork River to create the massive Glacial Lake Missoula hundreds of miles away in Montana. The ice dams burst repeatedly over thousands of years of melting and refreezing, each time sending cataclysmic floods through eastern Washington toward the Pacific Ocean.

Walls of water at least 1,000 feet deep and traveling 60 miles per hour entered the Columbia River and cut through the ancient basalt flows and the Cascade Range to carve the deep channel of the gorge. Monstrous boulders and gravel carried along in the waters scoured the cliff sides, and waterfalls now spill over the edges of the canyon where entire streams had their beds carved out from under them. Rockfalls and landslides still occur along the canyon walls, making the gorge a work in progress.

Catching the wind with transparent sails, wind surfers zoom across the surface of the gorge.

Boiling and Whorling

We fly over portions of the Columbia River that were impassible due to steep falls and rapids when Lewis and Clark came through. The natives had warned the explorers about the Great Falls of the Columbia, later called Celilo Falls, where several narrow channels divided the stream between islands of hard black rock. The Corps made a short but difficult portage around the falls.

Before the construction of locks and dams in the early- and mid-1900s and the resulting inundation of falls and rapids all along the river, the Great Falls of the Columbia was one of the region's best fishing sites and a meeting and

MARYHILL, WASHINGTON
Maryhill Museum of Art sits like a cultural oasis on a bluff above the Columbia River

WALLULA, WASHINGTON
On the brown hilltops, high-tech wind farms resemble squads of marching stick soldiers with swirling swords.

THE DALLES, OREGON

Resembling a wrinkled quilt, the orchards below made my mouth water thinking of the fresh cherries I had eaten the day before.

Leaving The Dalles early one morning, I head east, climbing above the canyon walls. Even though I had flown over here on the way west, looking down on the Columbia River with this different lighting and perspective gives me a new experience. Wanting to photograph the river canyon, I try to find a way to show the scale of the huge cliffs. Up ahead I spy a barge inching upstream against the current. Reducing power and pushing the stick forward, I indicate to *Cloud Chaser* I want this "elevator to go to the ground floor."

I complete the shot and then apply full power to climb out of the canyon. The first thing I notice is one of the RPM gauges drops to zero—the left engine has quit. *Cloud Chaser's* two engines are close to the centerline of the airframe, so if one goes out, the other provides thrust that is fairly centered, unlike large twin-engine planes that yaw sharply to one side when an engine fails. I instinctively use opposite rudder to keep the plane on course and continue my climbout at 500 feet per minute, setting a course for the nearest runway that is at least half an hour away.

I do a fast review of all the things I have been taught to do with an engine out. But *Cloud Chaser's* performance is hardly altered. As long as I keep hard right rudder, she flies with no problem. I land and am relieved to find it is only a fuel filter problem, not a major engine repair. In 10 minutes I'm airborne again. Because I often fly in isolated areas and at low altitudes, this is the only kind of aircraft that makes sense to me. If this had been a single engine plane, my only option would have been to swim to shore! The standard pilot's philosophy is "altitude is your friend," and although it's nice to have friends, these photos wouldn't have been possible with high altitude flying.

In my previous plane—a single engine experimental—my security blanket was a ballistic recovery chute. Since the plane was also amphibious, I could have glided to a graceful landing on this river without using the chute.

With this new experience under my belt, I now have ideas on how to improve the safety of *Cloud Chaser* even further. Perhaps I'll link the two fuel tanks together to improve my single engine range.

trading place for many tribes. A skillful fisherman could pull in 100 or more salmon a day using a dip net, and the fish were dried to preserve them for storage and trade.

Continuing downriver, the Corps had to face fearsome rapids they called "the Narrows," later known as The Dalles, a name derived from a French term for the long and flat rocks in the river. Here the churning river was confined in a narrow channel about 45 yards wide, but the canoes made it through. Clark wrote, "... I deturmined to pass through this place notwithstanding the horrid appearance of this

Trying for one last salmon during the final glow of sunshine, this native American uses a dip net in traditional Nez Perce style.

agitated gut Swelling, boiling & whorling in every direction ... however we passed Safe to the astonishment of all the Inds: of the last Lodges who viewed us from the top of the rock."

Harvests of salmon on the Columbia have declined precipitously over the past 80 years, but this evening, after landing at the town of The Dalles, we get a close-up view of how some native fishermen still ply their trade. Ron gets a sunset shot of a young Nez Perce man standing on a traditional-style wooden fishing scaffold that overhangs the water. We take a step back in time as Sean McConville shows us how he uses a 10-foot diameter dip net to pull in salmon as his people have done for thousands of years.

Wind and Water

We rise early, eat a quick breakfast, don fleece jackets and windbreakers, and strap ourselves into *Cloud Chaser* for a flight over the most dramatic part of the Columbia River Gorge. The Dalles is at the western edge of the hot and dry country of the Columbia Plains. Beyond it, the majestic canyon narrows, and the river moves with enormous energy. We soon cross the crest of the Cascade Range and enter the lush Pacific Forest. Here the land below us gets plenty of rain, and it's beautifully green and heavily timbered.

THE DALLES, OREGON
A tranquil lake now stands where torrents of cascading water once challenged salmon and men alike.

P O R T L A N D ,   O R E G O N

From the appearance of the geometrically perfect monoliths and the chatter on the radio, it's obvious we have reentered Metropolis, USA.

The sudden change from arid land to rainforest is a textbook example of how mountains affect climate. Moisture coming from the direction of the ocean travels eastward, rising and condensing over the Cascade Range, and falling as rain or snow on the western flanks of the mountains to create dense green forests. Beyond the crest of the mountains the eastern country lies in the "rain shadow" of the range, receiving very little moisture.

On the west side of the range, the riverside towns are small gems set in spruce, fir and cedar atop rocky cliffs at the water's edge. At the Hood River and Stephenson we must stay high to avoid the choppy winds that swirl between the canyon walls. Below us, in a realm we dare not enter, the funneled winds of the canyon provide a mecca for water sports. Windsurfers with diaphanous sails turn and twist in the white-capped waves. Kite-boarders dart, leap into the air and pirouette like multi-colored fireflies.

We're soon over the mammoth Bonneville Dam. The lake above it has submerged a dangerous rapid that Lewis and Clark called the "Great Shute." The Corps had to detour around the rapids, where the Cascade Indians controlled the route and extracted a tribute from river travelers.

Playing Above Portland

We emerge from the Gorge at its western end near Portland, Oregon, a bright city set in deep green forests with Mt. Hood as a backdrop. Friends have invited us to land at a residential airport. We head for their grass strip at Hillsboro, on the outskirts of Portland.

Cloud Chaser sets down softly on the thick turf, and we taxi right into Bill and Bette Jackson's backyard. Both of the Jacksons are pilots, and Bill is also a licensed airplane mechanic. Their garage is full of airplane parts, renovations in progress. Several of the neighbors in this airpark community come out to see the bright green flying canoe that has come across a continent.

In the morning Ron does some routine maintenance on the airplane, and then takes Bill for a ride. Bill has friends in the Hillsboro tower, and he wants to surprise and impress them with *Cloud Chaser*'s short field landing and takeoff capabilities. Ron is

A mosaic of colored cargo containers is a vivid reminder of our economic ties with the rest of the world.

happy to oblige. Landing the plane using just 100 feet of runway, he then zooms upward again at steep angle of climb, showing off a little. While Bill is overcome with laughter in the back seat, the controller in the tower coolly asks, "What kind of plane is that?" When Ron replies, "Just something I built at home," Bill lets out another whoop of laughter. He's having the time of his life.

Top of the World

Mt. Hood, the regal peak that Lewis and Clark saw only from a distance, beckons us to come closer. Leaving the buzz of the city behind, Ron and I ascend the forested slopes of the sleeping giant volcano, taking care to stay on the windward side where the breeze is strong but steady. We climb to 9,000 then 10,000 feet, near the craggy summit tinged with glaciers. In the distance we see the white tops of two more peaks of the Cascades, Mt. Adams to the north and Mt. Jefferson to the south.

The air is cold and pure, and we are alone in this high realm of austere, timeless beauty. We stay as long as we dare, and then I take the stick to start our descent while Ron changes lenses. He wants to capture the backlit haze gathering in the valleys as the sun slips down. It's been a magical evening at the top of the world.

River Becomes Ocean

The broad and long estuary of the Columbia spreads out beneath us in the morning. Container ships and tankers are skirting small islands as they head inland. The mouth of the Columbia is as wide as some lakes. Its tides can be felt 20 miles upriver where Clark mistakenly thought the Corps had reached the ocean shore and wrote: "Great joy in camp we are in *View* of the *Ocian* ...this great Pacific Octean which we been So long anxious to See."

Smelling the salt air, we soon reach the wide-open ocean, today only lightly shrouded in coastal fog, and land at Astoria, Oregon. The maritime town was founded just

(above) The 125-foot Astoria Column stands as a sentinel to passing freighters. Spiraling up the entire outside of the column, the mural (left) was created by Italian artist Atillio Pusterla. His detailed frieze depicts the westward expansion of settlers and Oregon's early history.

MOUNT HOOD, OREGON

The crown of Mt. Hood, accented with ice and snow, stands out boldly above the greenery that drapes like a veil across ancient lava flows.

Reenactor Sean Johnson, as Corps member Private Shannon, acts as a first-person interpreter, knowing only what has happened in his life before February 1806. He boils seawater to make salt for the return trip.

(right) Across America, Cloud Chaser's shadow has bathed in many streams and rivers. Now, with the Pacific Ocean below us, our shadow swims in a pool of blue as vast as half the earth.

four years after the Corps' visit, on the southern shore of the Columbia where the broad river spills into the Pacific.

Cloud Chaser has brought us safely to our outbound goal, and now the plane is parked beside an unusual variety of working aircraft. Small single-engine planes fitted with plexiglass doors are "fish-spotter" craft. Their pilots search for schools of fish in the open ocean and report the locations to commercial fishermen. Coast Guard helicopters stage daring rescue missions from here or deliver harbor pilots to ships approaching port.

In town, Victorian homes grace streets that encircle the steep hillsides. Nearly every evening a marine layer of coastal fog rolls ashore, softening the buildings and docks with a mysterious mist. We camp at the nearby town of Seaside and walk the beach at sundown. Ryan braves the chilly Pacific, just to be able to say he swam in every body of water that Lewis and Clark encountered on their trip.

Making Salt

Fort Clatsop is a replica of the Corps' home during the last winter of their journey. Here they survived a harsh season, seeing only 12 days without rain and only six days with a little sunshine. The fort flies a 15-star, 15-stripe flag like the one that Lewis and Clark carried.

Today is a gloriously sunny day, and the cedar forest around the fort is resplendent. We talk with Sean Johnson, a third-generation park ranger who has just grown into his dad's National Park Service uniform. Steeped in Lewis and Clark history since birth, he's worked with Stephen Ambrose, Ken Burns, and other Lewis and Clark interpreters of national stature. He invites us to attend a living history presentation at the Salt Works Camp on the beach at nearby Seaside, where he will play the role of Private Shannon.

We find the Corps' satellite camp on the beach where the men undertook the laborious process of boiling sea water to make salt for the return journey. A park ranger greets us and explains our mission: as visitors at the reenactment, we are to take on the role of Clatsop Indians, because the members of the Corps on the beach will not recognize any other sort of strangers approaching them.

The Astoria Bridge, one of man's most challenging creations, contrasts strongly with the delicate creations of nature.

(right) After 7,000 miles of following rivers, we cross a finish line marked only by a lonely lighthouse near Ilwaco, Washington. Like a giant glass beehive, the fresnel lens (left) focuses the beam of light coming from the lighthouse.

We've brought a bottle of wine as a trade item, and we offer it to "Private Field" who is roasting a duck on a spit over a wood fire. The private looks at the bottle quizzically, then opens it and pours the wine over the duck. He opens a pouch containing the few remaining trade goods of the Corps and hands us a few beads and small pieces of copper wire in exchange. We offer our dog, Jack, as a reenactor for Lewis's Newfoundland, Seaman, but Jack is a low-slung mixed breed and doesn't fit the profile.

"Sergeant Gass," the carpenter in charge of building Fort Clatsop and Fort Mandan, is sitting on a piece of driftwood, whittling a wooden handle for a knife blade. At age 35 he's a salty senior member of the Corps. He says he'll never marry and has little use for women, but we know from the history books that Gass went on to marry at age 60. He fathered many children and lived until his 99th year.

Leaving the Portland airspace, we receive permission from approach control to switch frequencies and travel on our VFR (Visual Flight Rules) course. Once again we are free to navigate as we wish. As we progress gradually downstream, the crew on a large ocean-going freighter waves as we pass overhead. The scent of freshly cut fir trees fills the air as we approach the Lewis and Clark Bridge at Longview. We drift over a logging terminal and watch as giant machines that resemble pincher ants move the logs from trucks and pile them in neat stacks by the dock.

Another 10 miles upriver the air becomes distinctly cooler and rougher. The GPS indicates that eight more miles ahead at our 10 o'clock position is the Astoria airport, meaning we need to stay on our toes to check for air traffic at this uncontrolled field. On the Washington side of the river, beside the bluffs, several wind surfers streak across the water like colorful insects. Although it's play for them, bucking this turbulence while trying to shoot photos is not fun for me. As we near the coast, the Astoria Bridge—one of man's most awesome structures— beckons to me to take its picture. Below us, seagulls fly beside the roadway as if they are challenging the cars to a race.

Now that we can see the Pacific Ocean, our excitement is hard to contain. This must be as close as we can get to feeling what Lewis and Clark felt. For a month and a half we traveled over 7,000 miles, following rivers and streams. We observed as they snaked through the flat land of the prairie, tumbled over canyon walls and joined with their cousins to gather strength for the march to the sea. Sometimes swift, sometimes slow, those many miles of rivers now seem like only a trickle of water compared to the vastness of the world's largest ocean before us.

With *Cloud Chaser*'s nose pointing west into the wind, we sit at near-hover speed 500 feet above the inlet, relishing this moment. It's about an hour before sundown, so we bank to the right to find the perfect angle for the lighthouse at Cape Disappointment. Soaring slowly

Sunset at North Head lighthouse in Ilwaco, Washington.

by the lighthouse and cliffs, I can relate to the seagulls just off our wingtip. My favorite story when I was young was a book called *Jonathan Livingston Seagull*. Although the plot was simple, the self-appointed challenges and freedom the seagull experienced were the same things I wanted out of life.

It's strange how people are drawn to these icons that cling to the jagged cliffs. Lighthouses have actually been made obsolete by GPS. Using satellites, ships now know their own position plus or minus a few feet anywhere on the planet.

Turning south we follow the shoreline to Canon Beach in hopes of getting a shot of Haystack Rock before we lose the light. Hundreds of birds are starting to roost on the rock ledges at Bird Point as we pass by. In the water beneath us, two porpoises run parallel to the shoreline, as if they are leading us to our destination.

As we draw closer to Haystack Rock the low evening sun accents the many colors and textures on its western face. The bold white seagulls that speckle the rock look like dandruff on my otherwise flawless canvas. Even though I'm confident the best shot is preserved in the camera, I can't let go of this final scene of the day. Knowing that no photo is perfect, I continue searching for a better angle until the sun's last ray.

After stowing the camera beside the seat, I initiate a turn to the northeast and start our climb over the cliffs towards Astoria. On the way to the airport we have time to relax and talk about what an incredible day this has been.

It's interesting how all these instruments and gauges in the cockpit help me find my way and keep me safe. Perhaps I should count the camera as a survival tool as well. Without it, I would surely die an agonizing death from guilt and frustration, unable to preserve forever what I have seen.

Twelve Tribes

To learn more about the native people who lived along the coast and the Columbia River for thousands of years before the Lewis and Clark Expedition, we meet Cliff Snider, Chief Gray Wolf, a retired chief of the Chinook tribe, at his home in Portland.

When Lewis and Clark reached the Columbia, natives all along the river received word of the party's arrival by "canoe telegraph and moccasin Western Union," Chief Snider says. Twelve tribes along the Columbia, including the Clatsops, spoke Chinookan languages. Chief Snider's fourth great-grandfather, Chief Comcomly, greeted Lewis and Clark at the coast. The Chinook people provided food for the Corps

and helped them locate a favorable site for Fort Clatsop.

Chief Snider has been involved at the national level in planning the Bicentennial. He tells us that many Native Americans did not want to call the event a "celebration" because although Lewis and Clark came in peace, their exploration of the West presaged U.S. exploitation of native lands and suppression of native cultures. National organizers agreed that the Bicentennial would instead be called a "commemoration" of the historical event. Although the U.S. government has recently revoked the Chinooks' official recognition as a tribe, the Chinook people are taking an active part in Bicentennial events.

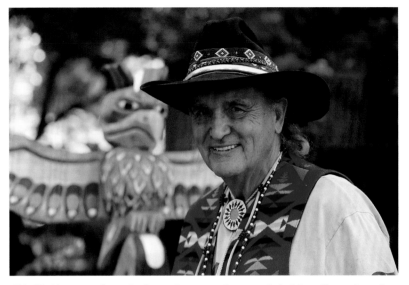

Chief Snider poses for us in front of a totem that stands in his well-manicured lawn. "Walls of fame" in his garage are covered in memorabilia, athletic medals and family pictures.

On a wet Christmas Eve day in 1805 the Corps of Discovery moved into a stockade fort and prepared to spend the winter. Fort Clatsop was named in honor of the local Clatsop people. Interlocking logs (left) in the wall of Fort Clatsop form an abstract pattern.

LONGVIEW, WASHINGTON

Like icons of the Northwest, log piles await departure to other parts of the world. The Lewis and Clark Bridge connects Oregon with Washington.

COLUMBIA RIVER GORGE, OREGON

Our journey half completed, the rising sun now points the way home.

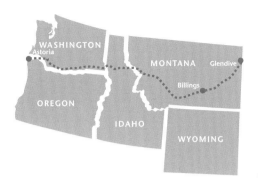

CHAPTER NINE

Homeward Bound: Then and Now

FOR THE FIRST TIME IN TWO MONTHS, *CLOUD CHASER* heads east. We're pointed roughly toward home, but there's no on/off switch for wanderlust in this airplane, and by now we have a finely honed desire to discover new places and people.

Lewis and Clark also wanted to explore new territory on their return trip. They even made the risky decision to split the party so that they could survey both the Marias River and the Yellowstone River. Just south of Missoula at Traveler's Rest, the two Captains parted company, intending to meet again at where the Yellowstone and the Missouri join. We'll follow the route of Clark and his party across Montana.

We've spent a week retracing our path in the sky along the Washington/Oregon border and across southeastern Washington to Lewiston, Idaho. Now we're over the heavily forested Lolo Trail again, this time on an eastbound crossing of the Bitterroot Range. The air is silky smooth but a bit hazy. The summer season of wildfires has started, and it's quite severe this year. In the distance to the south we see smoke from fires in the mountains.

We land at Missoula, a city at the hub of five valleys, at the confluence of the northward-flowing Bitterroot River and the westward-flowing Clark Fork River. By volume, the Clark Fork is the largest river in Montana.

This stunning area was shaped by fault zones, by Glacial Lake Missoula and by numerous ice ages. The mountains east of the city are terraced by horizontal benches that mark the successive shorelines of the mammoth glacial lake, and huge

It appears this Indian overslept while his tribe moved on.

Seeing this field outside of Bozeman we wondered if farmers create these patterns to catch our attention.

FORSYTH, MONTANA

From our aerial perch, we see features of the land that Clark and his men seldom viewed as they traveled along the river.

After an hour of flying along the Yellowstone River, I land at Livingston, tie down the plane and then notice a fire service helicopter landing and a fire crew setting up camp on an adjacent field.

It's the late summer fire season in a very dry Montana. Using our internet link, we have been closely monitoring the red dots on the map that indicate TFRs (Temporary Flight Restrictions) for forest fires. A dozen red dots signify areas to avoid because of the aerial traffic of smoke jumpers. To the south I can see smoke billowing between peaks in a distant valley.

My chase crew arrives, and we agree to set up camp because of deteriorating weather. Large storm clouds are forming to the north. While we're setting up camp, activity at the airport quickly increases to a frenzied pace. A large crane helicopter arrives with its support crew and tanker truck. It can dump about 3,000 gallons of water from a huge bucket carried on a long sling, but the water seems like a thimble-full when it's dropped over thousands of blazing acres. Soon, three more helicopters with scoops, snorkels and buckets join the fire detail. Fire crews from California and Arizona have driven in by the truckload.

Over on the tarmac we visit with the crew of a twin-engine fire spotter plane that has just landed. Even though a tremendous storm is brewing, they are preparing to take off again immediately to direct the helicopters to the hot spots.

In the distance we can see sheets of rain descending, but the moisture never reaches the ground. Instead, bolts of dry lightning are hitting all around us. This is the firefighting crew's biggest worry. It's as if Mother Nature is taunting them by randomly tossing lit matches. As we watch the storm, a bolt of lightning strikes the top of a distant mesa. Within seconds smoke begins to spiral upward. Ryan runs to tell the fire crew, and they quickly send a team to work it.

A helicopter pilot, a big guy with a full bushy beard, lands and climbs out of his chopper. Shaking his head, he exclaims, "That lighting was hitting within a hundred feet of me. Time to get the hell out of there!"

As darkness falls, the canyons in the distance glow with the orange of the wild fires. I'm concerned about being able to leave the next day. Surely a big red dot is on the map at Livingston right now, forcing the traffic to bypass the airport.

In the morning the storms have passed with only a few drops of rain falling on the airport. I find the chief of operations and explain our mission. He graciously allows me to take off, and I head to the east.

Near Three Forks we see an unusual folded texture of the mountains.

boulders lie where they were dropped from icebergs that floated in the lake. The grand scale of the natural scenery dwarfs downtown Missoula, but the city is lively on a summer evening. At a waterfront park, we ride horses, unicorns and lions on a colorful carousel that's the pride of the town.

Another Flying Canoe

Early in the morning, *Cloud Chaser* climbs above the sleeping city of Missoula, and for a few miles we're over Lewis' eastward route of departure from the area. Below us the Clark Fork River spills out of a narrow gap between two mountains. Shoshones and other natives told Lewis of a shortcut to the Great Falls, and he set out through the gap below us with nine of his men and five Indian guides. We soon diverge from Lewis' path and turn southeastward, cutting a diagonal to reach Clark's trail along the Yellowstone River.

Following the Clark Fork River upstream towards Butte, the oddly shaped hills are tilted and grooved, and we're in backcountry again. The small airport at Butte is perched at 5,500 feet, and today something unusual is going on.

Nearly a hundred people are roaming the ramp area amid a colorful collection of airplanes. Ron makes a perfect landing and taxis to a parking spot flanked by an

MISSOULA, MONTANA

The tranquil mountain town is famous for flying aces and smoke jumpers.

Mining icons of Butte's past now sit idle like tombstones to attract the tourist.

assortment of antique aircraft, each one polished to a shine. *Cloud Chaser* has inadvertently arrived in the middle of an airshow, and a friendly local pilot tells us this is part of Butte's annual Evel Knievel Daze celebration. Suddenly the crowd gravitates toward the bright green plane. *Cloud Chaser* has become the top draw.

We're hungry and tired, but this is too much fun to miss. We stand for an hour beside the plane and answer the questions of crew-cut kids and grandmothers alike: "How fast does it fly? Does your dog go flying? You flew this all the way from Tennessee? What do you do when it rains?" People also want to know if we use bottled oxygen when flying high in mountainous areas, but we'd only need to do that for extended flights above 12,500 feet.

Just as the crowd begins to thin, a yellow twin of *Cloud Chaser* lands and pulls up next to us. The two guys flying in it, a father and son, are from Topeka, Kansas, and they're on a "mission" also. They plan to visit the dam the father helped construct in Wyoming. The local folks can't believe this rendezvous hasn't been planned, but we insist it's just coincidence. Thousands of small factory-built airplanes are flying in the world but only about a hundred planes like *Cloud Chaser*, and the odds against this sort of chance meeting are astronomical.

In town we learn that Evel Knievel, a man often considered a living American icon, is Butte's most famous

An old wagon wheel is now at rest in the mining museum in Butte.

BOZEMAN, MONTANA

As the sun begins to set, the Gallatin River shows no sign of haste. Its destiny to donate its resources to the Missouri River can surely wait another day.

A serene meadow near Three Forks, Montana, shows where hunters once drove thunderous herds of buffalo over the cliffs.

resident. Although he's best known for his daredevil stunts, he's also been an amazing athlete, a successful advocate for wilderness and a generous philanthropist. He grew up here, he's been a loyal supporter of his hometown, and his fellow citizens are mightily fond and proud of him.

Amid the historic brick buildings of the hilly downtown, they've scheduled a motorcycle car-jumping event in the afternoon, followed by evening festivities that are introduced by Evel Knievel himself. We join the dancing in the streets, to the sound of the "Bop-a-Dips" band. I am amazed that our teenaged Ryan knows all the words to the oldies songs they play. Having descended into some sort of midsummer madness in Montana, we stay up late with the local revelers, going on adrenaline. A fireworks display gets out of hand and starts a grass fire in the block next to where we've parked our truck, but the fire brigade has been standing by. Everything quickly returns to normal, or to whatever is considered normal for this friendly and crazy town.

In the aftermath of wind and pounding rain, the mighty storm salutes Cloud Chaser's *bravery with a rainbow.*

POMPEYS PILLAR, MONTANA

Clark's self-made monument is named for Sacagawea's small son whom he had nicknamed "Little Pomp." On July 25, 1805, Clark carved his name and the date into the rock's soft sandstone surface. The pillar also has Native American drawings and other historical descriptions on it.

The next day we visit the World Museum of Mining and learn how Butte earned the nickname "the Richest Hill on Earth." For more than a century, the area yielded a wealth of copper, lead and silver ore. Huge steel towers—"head frames" for elevator shafts in the mines—stand prominently around the town. The last mine closed in 1983, after decades of declining copper prices. Much of the land impacted by mining has been restored, and a massive cleanup of mining contaminants in the Clark Fork River is now in the final planning stages.

Where There's Smoke...

For three weeks there's been no break in the heat and no rain. In the relative cool of early morning, we fly out of Butte, looking deep into the mile-wide Berkeley Pit mine on the east side of town, and then push on toward our next stop at Bozeman. We cross sharply ribbed mountainsides and skim over the broad valley at Three Forks, with high ranges all around in the distance.

Flying over the Gallatin River and its small tributaries, we see steam rising from small ponds fed by natural hot springs. Hundreds of white pelicans float on the river and deer graze in the marshy areas. The wilderness scenery is positively idyllic.

We land at Belgrade, near Bozeman. Later in the evening we fly over a field where the farmer has planted a new crop in a complex geometric pattern, apparently just for fun. We salute his artistry with a tip of our wings.

Suddenly, the light dims eerily and the wind picks up. A peculiar wall of monolithic clouds obscures the setting sun and spans half of the horizon. At the airfield we're told that the cloud we see is a wall of smoke from a new wildfire to the southwest. For nearly two months, no rain has fallen in the arid parts of Montana. Dry lightning has started more than 30 fires around the state.

(above) The Yellowstone River coupled with the steel highway of the railroad brings life to this otherwise desert community of Glendive, Montana.

(left) Ignoring the compass, Cloud Chaser *knows only allegiance to the river and its many bends.*

(above) A vivid splash of color on a huge plain, Fort Union is located near the juncture of the Missouri and Yellowstone Rivers. In its heyday, this trading post, considered "the grandest fort on the Missouri," was the fulfillment of Jefferson's vision to open the West to commerce. Located in an ideal spot to draw many tribes, the Fort's primary medium of exchange was buffalo.

(right) Looking down at the restored Fort Union that sits beside the retreating Missouri River, it's difficult to imagine that paddlewheelers once regularly docked right at the front door, delivering passengers and goods from the East.

Over the Yellowstone River

Near the site of present-day Livingston, Clark and his party intersected the Yellowstone River, which Clark called the *Rochejhone*, from the French term for the yellow rocks exposed in the river valley. The Yellowstone originates in northwest Wyoming, southeast of Yellowstone National Park. It feeds and drains Yellowstone Lake within the park, then enters Montana to pass over rugged falls and through a spectacular canyon and a narrow valley until it reaches a relatively open area around the town of Livingston.

Our next stop is at Billings, a busy financial center. Although it's the largest city in Montana, its population is only about 90,000. The city is decorated with vintage signs in neon and metal. Public art and beautiful downtown landscaping give it an upscale atmosphere.

We meet Tom Scott, CEO of First Interstate Bank. Tom, chairman of the Montana Lewis and Clark Legacy Campaign, is a fellow pilot. He tells us that the Bicentennial is bringing a lot of visitors to Montana, where the Corps of Discovery spent the greatest number of days on the trail. "Many areas remain much the same as when Lewis and Clark saw them," he says. Tom flies a jet, but he'd enjoy the view of the trail we get from *Cloud Chaser*. "I fly higher than you," he says, "but I don't get to see it the way you do."

In the morning it's my turn to fly *Cloud Chaser* again to pose for air-to-air photos. Ron has again rented a second plane as a photography platform. The light is perfect, but the air is a bit choppy. We'll find it hard to maneuver the two planes into stable positions. After a 15-minute discussion and a short test flight, we decide it's worth a try.

Heading west over the river, the landscape is exquisitely shaped by sculpted cliffs. "Hold your altitude right there," Ron's voice intones on the radio from the small Cessna, but it's a feat easier said than done. Somehow, with the two planes bucking at random, Ron gets some shots that are book-cover material. We return to base pleased with our work.

Pompeys Pillar

Soaring eastward over the river the next day, we come upon the prominent rock formation Captain Clark called "Pompy's Tower." Clark named the landmark in honor of Sacagawea's 18-month-old son Jean Baptiste, whom he had fondly nicknamed "little Pomp." Clark cut his own name and the date into the rock next to some Indian drawings. The inscription still visible today is the only remaining physical evidence of the expedition that can be seen on the trail, and the site is now Pompeys Pillar National Monument.

Soon we move past centuries-old history to futuristic sculpture. The Makoshika badlands stretch along the riverbank, their bizarre pillars standing like props from a science fiction movie. Hard caps of erosion-resistant sandstone sit atop vertical columns of mudstone that have weathered into alien shapes.

Two hours northeast is Miles City, another wonderful small town. Main Street has retained much of its "Old West" atmosphere, and the Range Riders Museum is a gem, with an eclectic collection of barbed wire, fort dioramas and cowboy boots with their owners' pictures mounted above each well-worn pair.

It's still hot, even after sundown, and in the middle of the night a howling wind wakens us. Ron and Sue dash to the airport and find that a 45-mph gale is playing havoc with *Cloud Chaser*. Since they've already used all their ropes, they hold onto the tail tightly for almost an hour, while blowing grit and sand sting their legs. Two local policemen see them as they cruise by on their rounds, and soon three patrol cars are coming across the tarmac toward them. They explain the situation, and officers are eager to help. They manage to find some ropes in a search-and-rescue hangar on the field, and the plane is tied down more securely.

White pelicans float above the trees like confetti blown by the wind.

Red Carpet Treatment

We receive a warm welcome the next day when we set down at the airport near Glendive. It's clear that the manager, Leon Baker, treats all his visitors well. He keeps a freezer full of TV dinners and corn dogs for hungry travelers. He tells us he is "an agent for the paper" and asks our permission to call a reporter out to interview Ron and the crew. In this quiet corner of Montana, our little green airplane is big news.

At McDonald's at lunchtime, we overhear a group of local residents who are socializing over ice cream sundaes. "Did you see that green ultralight this afternoon?" "Yeah, it had two engines, and it was flyin' real slow!" After a few more comments, we can't resist introducing ourselves and telling the story of our trip. We invite our new friends to come to the airport to see the "big green twin." In the evening, while we are camped at the airport, a crowd comes to see the plane.

After our gracious airport host provides us breakfast, we follow the Yellowstone to Fairview, a small town near the Missouri and Yellowstone Rivers. The airport consists of one dirt strip and a locked hangar. Several cropduster planes sit waiting for duty. We made the sole flight in and out of this remote spot where we "boondocked" overnight.

Clark called the Yellowstone a "delightful" river, and the stream is still undammed and free-flowing 200 years later. In the summer growing season, irrigation takes a heavy toll on it, and today the water level looks very low. At the mouth of the Yellowstone we rejoin our old friend the Missouri, which will lead us toward home.

NEAR SIDNEY, MONTANA

At their confluence, the Yellowstone and Missouri Rivers join forces to begin a journey to the Gulf of Mexico over a thousand miles away.

LIVINGSTON, MONTANA
With the Rockies now behind us, we leave our mountain-flying adventures and allow the Yellowstone River to show us the way home.

FORSYTH, MONTANA
Graceful cottonwoods dot the otherwise brown landscape.

SIDNEY, MONTANA

With formations so rich in color and texture, should they really deserve to be called "badlands?"

N E A R   S I D N E Y ,   M O N T A N A

The Yellowstone River surrenders its wealth to a patchwork of fields to feed the hungry.

CHAPTER TEN

In the "Red-Haired Doctor's Town"

ON THEIR RETURN TRIP, THE CORPS OF DISCOVERY TRAVELED THE MISSOURI from its confluence with the Yellowstone River in present-day North Dakota to St. Louis in about six weeks time, though the journey upstream had taken them more than five months. At the Mandan villages, they found that their winter fort of 1804-1805 had accidentally burned, and little was left to mark their sojourn there. A Mandan leader, Chief Big White, and his family consented to travel to St. Louis with the Captains and later to Washington, DC, to visit President Jefferson.

As they proceeded down river, Lewis and Clark met traders who informed them that since they had received no communication from the Captains in more than a year, most Americans had given the company up as lost. The Corps returned to St. Louis in September 1806, amid much cheering, congratulations and joyous celebration with old friends. They had accomplished much and returned home safely.

Sacagawea, Charbonneau and their son, Jean Baptiste, remained at the Mandan villages, but Captain Clark offered to raise and educate the boy. Indeed a few years later the parents brought Jean Baptiste to St. Louis for that purpose. Clark became Jefferson's superintendent of Indian affairs, and he lived and worked in St. Louis until his death in 1838. The city became known

(above) A doe and fawn pause for a late evening drink of water.

(left) Our imaginations now nourished by our experiences, we return to St. Louis, Gateway to the West, to share our treasure of knowledge.

For the past month the land we have seen was mostly dependent upon the river for nourishment. Here the moisture-laden clouds treat the land more fairly.

WHITING, IOWA

This small Iowa town looks as though it sprouted from an acorn that bounced off a passing train.

as "the red-haired Doctor's town" in his honor, memorializing the nickname he earned though his medical treatment of natives during the expedition.

Full Circle in Cloud Chaser

Descending the Missouri, we revisit some of our outbound stops and receive hearty second welcomes from people we had met a few months before. "Most folks pass through going just one way on the Lewis and Clark trail," a volunteer at Lewis and Clark State Park in Iowa tells us. "We're surprised to see you again." We happily tell about our adventures of the summer. Then we return to the St. Louis area, our starting point of nearly three months ago, not wanting our journey to end but proud of our successful full-circle aerial adventure.

Landing at St. Charles Airport just outside St. Louis, a frenzy of activity is taking place at the small airfield, and several planes are with us in the traffic pattern. A popular flight school is based here and a lot of local flyers use the airport, but the runways have grass growing on them and things are a bit shabby. We're told that the airport has trouble competing with the larger public fields for funding.

Ron wants to shoot more photos of St. Louis because on our outbound trip the city was draped in haze. This time we face new challenges. Tonight's a major league baseball game going on, so a three-mile-radius flight restriction around Busch Stadium keeps us away from the Arch and the downtown area. We take off when the game is nearly finished, circle around until the flight restriction is dropped, then move in toward the city. By this time the light is a bit lower than optimum. Finally, the next morning perseverance pays off, and Ron gets a photo that is a beautiful farewell tribute to St. Louis.

Even though many of my friends and relatives think I cheat death on a daily basis, it's just another day at the office for me as I touch down in late evening.

I am a part of all that I have met;
Yet all experience is an arch wherethro'
Gleams that untravel'd world whose margin fades
For ever and for ever when I move.
                    —*Ulysses*, Alfred, Lord Tennyson

It's time for us to leave the trail, but the joys, memories and lessons of our long journey will stay with us always. Our adventure has left indelible impressions on our minds and hearts—the kaleidoscopic colors of the fields and cities we've seen from above, the warmth and vitality of today's Americans we have met on the land.

In late afternoon we sit on the cool white marble steps of Captain Clark's tomb, quietly communing with William. He lies surrounded by members of his family on a serene hill overlooking St. Louis. His friend and colleague, Captain Lewis, lies along the Natchez Trace in Tennessee, where his life was ended, probably by his own hand, just three years after the expedition's return.

We ponder the tremendous journey the members of the Corps of Discovery made and the events they witnessed during their lives. The Louisiana Purchase opened the gate to the West, and frontiersmen and settlers began to push across the continent even before the Corps returned to St. Louis. Just 63 years after Lewis and Clark's journey ended, the Transcontinental Railroad was completed, allowing people and goods to cross the entire country in four-days time. Neither of the Captains lived to see that happen, but Sergeant Gass, who survived to age 99, did.

Talking with Native Americans whose ancestors inhabited the land when Lewis and Clark passed through, and with ranchers and farmers whose families came later to seek livelihoods and new opportunities, we glimpsed a larger reality than history books can ever describe. The voices of our own contemporaries have made histories and cultures come alive.

It's clear that the West was far from being an empty wilderness when Lewis and Clark began their explorations. The many tribes the Corps encountered had developed skilled ways of living off the land, and on many occasions the Corps might not have survived without their help. Lewis and Clark traveled trails that were part of extensive hunting and trade routes established by the Indians, and both the networks and trade goods were critically important to U.S. and European powers.

The Anglo-American mindset of the early 1800s was little disposed to recognize or appreciate the diverse social systems and religions that Native Americans had developed over thousands of years, but Americans can be proud that, for the most part, Lewis and Clark seemed to be respectful of differences they did not understand. Later the U.S.

Standing as a relentless monument in every storm, Haystack Rock is an enduring symbol of the epic achievements of Lewis and Clark and the Corps of Discovery. Flying thousands of miles to the Pacific coast (above) and back, we've come full circle, returning to the Gateway Arch in St. Louis (right).

St. Louis, Missouri

With the Mississippi River as our final goal line we float to victory with our treasure trove of knowledge and images.

sought to subdue or conquer many tribes in the name of westward expansion and Manifest Destiny. In spite of all that happened, native tribes have kept their traditions and knowledge alive, and they add much depth and richness to the mosaic of American life today. We value the experiences we've had with tribe members, and we're inspired by their past and present contributions to our nation.

In this Bicentennial year of the Lewis and Clark Expedition, and the Centennial year of the Wright brothers' First Flight at Kitty Hawk, we're thrilled with our exciting aerial exploration. Although we used modern technology, we tapped into a timeless spirit of adventure. Because we made our journey in a way that was personally challenging for us, we feel a strong connection to the courageous and resourceful explorers who preceded us 200 years ago. We can relate to their labors and joys. We can begin to see our nation through their eyes and appreciate the monumental consequences of their accomplishments. The scenes we've glimpsed and photographed will call us to return and explore further for years to come, and it seems we've only scratched the surface of the rich history, mysteries and controversies that surround the expedition and the events that came afterward. We're inspired to continue to learn more.

Although we had studied our route extensively before our trip, we are astounded at the beauty and wonder of the country we've seen. The variety of landforms and rivers along this one route across America seems infinite. Often within a single state we found semi-deserts and rich dense forests, rocky badlands and marshes full of waterfowl. Although development has taken its toll on many

beautiful natural areas, we learned that new and better-informed conversations about the management of natural resources are occurring in many places, hopefully with good effect for the future.

Our trip was incredibly rewarding for us personally. Ron and I, Sue and Ryan and our part-time ground crew drivers have had a wonderful adventure, and we've expanded our own fields of vision in many ways. We have explored the skies and seen the land from the air, with new eyes. A mystique still surrounds flying that stems from its millennia-old standing as the "ultimate impossibility." Everyone who flew in *Cloud Chaser* found that the experience transformed their notions of what is possible for them, and they now seem unstoppable in whatever they choose to do.

Flying low and slow over the landscape has changed how we look at our world. A friend who traveled home on an airliner after flying with Ron said that, for the first time, her attention was riveted to the scenes below throughout the long trip. Wherever she saw a river, she couldn't take her eyes off the water, which seemed to her a living thing. She wondered where each stream comes from, where it goes, and what history and future belong to it.

"Many voices, one journey" is a phrase being used to describe Americans' experience of the Lewis and Clark Bicentennial. As Ron and I commit our photos and thoughts to paper, we add our voices to many others that speak of the excitement, meaning and metaphor of the Lewis and Clark history. We thank all who have helped us and all who have told us their stories. We join them in their bright hopes and dreams for America in the next 200 years.

Sunset on the Oregon Coast.

Photographer's Notes: **The Ethereal Experience of Flight**

Long before we left home, I did extensive research to study the photographic possibilities. I spent so much time looking at topographic maps and satellite images of our route that I began to worry that the journey itself would hold no surprises. Once we were actually flying the trail, this concern evaporated. The flat detail shown on maps was no match for the real thing. The lighting, color and textures of the real American terrain revealed the soul of the country.

Until I traveled for three months above the riverbanks, sandbars and bends of so many rivers, I could not grasp the magnitude of these mighty waterways. As I reached the headwaters of Three Forks, Montana, seemingly endless mountain ranges rose to the west. I now understood the frustration Lewis and Clark must have felt, seeing these mountains stretch out before them.

For two years we studied the Lewis and Clark expedition, but it was only seeing every one of those countless snags that finally made the Corps' daily struggles real to me. Climbing a rocky overlook, I thought about the many moccasins that were worn thin. Even though their trail has long grown cold, the pain of their hardships still echoed within the canyon walls.

The experience of having their feet leave the ground is the one thing pilots have in common. Beyond that, interests vary widely. Some are fascinated with antique aircraft, some like being surrounded by instruments and many others like to go as fast as they can from point A to point B. When I first started flying kit-built experimental aircraft, my main objective was to explore and do photography. At that time I had no idea how aviation was going to impact me as an artist. It took lots of hours for me to get comfortable flying thousands of feet above the ground in this thing that resembles a canoe. Even now, after thousands of hours of flight, I occasionally have anxious moments. Fortunately, they only momentarily interrupt the ethereal experience of flight.

Many times I have been startled and caught off balance by people's questions about flying. One day I was telling the story about how we used a ranchers grass strip in the middle of nowhere and the question came up, "Who gives you the permission to take off?" "No one, because no one cares," I replied. This convinced me that a lot people aren't aware of the degree of freedom I experience when flying in the wilderness. People frequently ask me how I can fly and shoot photos at the same time. Most of the time when I shoot I'm at least 800

Sunset at 9,000 feet above the clouds.

feet above the ground. The closer you get to the subject the tougher it is to eliminate blur from movement.

Letting go of the stick momentarily to get a quick shot is not that dangerous because I have plenty of time to correct any problems. In areas of heavy air traffic a copilot is most essential. The copilot relieves you of radio work and helps keep an eye out for traffic.

As we draw to the end of our amazing journey, many things come to mind. How will we cope with the regular routines of our everyday life after experiencing the "call of the wild"? For the past three months I have flown over landscapes that never repeated but evolved like the view through a slowly rotating kaleidoscope. It wasn't like traveling to a destination. It was like *Cloud Chaser* was eagerly taking me to another valley to show what she had found. The visual rewards were so great that rolling out of bed and into the cockpit at 5 a.m. never bothered me. The eye candy of the scenery, supplemented with the almonds I kept beside the seat, could nourish me for hours. Faced with a constant barrage of possible compositions for my camera, the early morning chill only heightened my senses.

Imagine floating above the clouds at 9,000 feet at 40 mph The sound of moving air is negligible and the engines are close to idle. As the sun slowly sets, the clouds beneath start to glow in one hue and then another. It's like taking Beethoven's Ninth intravenously. After completing my shots I begin my descent at 500 feet per minute. What was a dry and cool 48 degrees above the clouds, transitions to warmth and deep shadows below my orange flower garden. Even if I found another shot, my lens was now fogged over from the increasing humidity. Approaching the airport in near total darkness, I click my mike button and activate the runway lights. The deserted darkness now turns into a glowing welcome mat.

Recalling unique moments above a lighthouse facing the ocean or floating above hundreds of buffalo on the prairie, I wish I could just press "replay." Being able to fly the plane slowly is wonderful, but it's seldom slow enough.

Although airports are the perfect place to groom your feathers and roost for the night, *Cloud Chaser* prefers to feel the wind against her wings than the earth touching her wheels. After three months following these watery highways, my understanding of this country is much richer—it has become a part of me in ways I could never have imagined. The land is in my blood now. I can't wait for the next adventure.

HEADING HOME
As the fog gives way to the sun, the dew on the trees sparkles in the light.

Acknowledgments

First of all, the authors would like to thank our spouses: Sue Lowery for her excellent design, her participation in our journey and her unfailing encouragement, and Skip Walker for his management of the home front and his enthusiastic support of our labors. We are grateful to Ryan Lowery, Anne Harman, Skip Walker, Anne Magee and Alan Walker, our part-time driver/companions on the journey; Bill Cushman, for historical review; Charlie Clark, Mark Shaw and Bruce Sanford for publishing guidance; Alan Walker for compiling the appendix; Anne Harman, Skip Walker, Kay Thrasher, and Nancy Neal for manuscript review; Roger and Tonny Blair, Bill and Bette Jackson, Doug and Cora Peterson, Manny Red Bear, Clyde Robinson and his family, Chief Cliff Snider, Leon Baker, and Gene Martin, our hosts along the trail; and numerous others who offered assistance of many kinds along our route.

Thanks to Reed Brown, Tom Boggs and folks at MotoSAT for our link to the outside world, and Phil Lockwood with ROTAX for offering to come bail us out anywhere in the country if the engines malfunctioned.

Major Sites of Interest

MISSOURI AND ILLINOIS

Jefferson National Memorial
11 North Fourth Street
St. Louis, Missouri 63102
Tel: 314-655-1700
www.nps.gov/jeff/

Lewis and Clark Center
701 Riverside Drive
St. Charles, Missouri 63301
Tel: 636-947-3199
www.lewisandclark.state.mo.us
/stcharles.asp

Camp DuBois at Wood River
Routes 3 and 143
Wood River, Illinois
Phone 618-254-1993
www.greatriverroad.com/Cities/Wood/
duboisLandmark.htm

Historic Fort Osage
Jackson Co. Parks and Recreation
Heritage Museums
105 Osage Street
Sibley, Missouri 64088
Tel: 816-650-5737
www.historicfortosage.com

NEBRASKA

Missouri River Basin—Lewis and Clark Interpretive Trail
Visitor's Center and Foundation
911 Central Avenue
Nebraska City, Nebraska 68410
Tel: 402-873-3388
www.mrb-lewisandclarkcenter.org

Fort Atkinson State Historical Park
US 75, one mile east of Fort Calhoun
PO Box 240
Fort Calhoun, Nebraska 68023
Tel: 402-468-5611
www.ngpc.state.ne.us/parks/

IOWA

Western Historic Trails Center
3434 Richard Downing Avenue
Council Bluffs, Iowa 51501
Tel: 712-366-4900
www.iowahistory.org/sites/
western_trails/western_trails.html

Lewis and Clark Monument and Scenic Overlook
19962 Monument Road
Council Bluffs, Iowa
Tel: 712-328-4650

Keelboat "Discovery"
Lewis and Clark State Park
I-29, Exit 112, Onawa, Iowa
Tel: 712-423-2829
www.lewisandclark2004.org

Lewis and Clark Interpretive Center
I-29, Exit 149
(Hamilton Boulevard) Sioux City, Iowa
Tel: 712-224-5242
www.siouxcitylcic.com

Sergeant Floyd Monument
1000 Larsen Park Road
Sioux City, Iowa
Tel: 712-279-0198
www.cr.nps.gov/nr/travel/lewisandclark/
ser.htm

Sergeant Floyd River Museum and Welcome Center
1000 Larson Park Road
Sioux City, Iowa
Tel: 712-279-0198
www.sioux-city.org/museum

SOUTH DAKOTA

Calumet Bluff/Gavins Point Dam Lewis and Clark Visitor Center
U.S. Army Corps of Engineers
PO Box 710
Yankton, South Dakota 57078
Tel: 402-667-7873, ext. 3246
www.nwo.usace.army.mil/html/
Lake_Proj/gavinspoint
visit.html

NORTH DAKOTA

Fort Abraham Lincoln State Park
4480 Fort Lincoln Road
Mandan, North Dakota 58554
Tel: 701-667-6340
www.ndparks.com/Parks/FLSP.htm

Fort Mandan
North Dakota Lewis and Clark
Bicentennial Foundation/Interpretive
Center
PO Box 607
Washburn, North Dakota 58577
Tel: 701-462-8535/877-462-8535
www.fortmandan.com

Knife River Indian Villages
National Historic Site
PO Box 9
Stanton, North Dakota 58571
Tel: 701-745-3309
www.nps.gov/knri/

Three Tribes Museum
PO Box 147
New Town, North Dakota 58763
Tel: 701-627-4477

MONTANA

Pompeys Pillar
Pompeys Pillar Visitor Center
I-94, Exit 23/State Hwy 312
Billings, Montana
Tel: 406-875-2233
www.mt.blm.gov/pillarmon/general.html

Lewis and Clark National Historic Trail Interpretive Center
4201 Giant Springs Road
PO Box 1806
Great Falls, Montana 59403
Tel: 406-727-8733
www.fs.fed.us/r1/lewisclark/lcic/

Gates of the Mountains
PO Box 478
Helena, Montana 59624
Tel: 406-458-5241
www.gatesofthemountains.com

Missouri Headwaters State Park
Hwy 286 off Hwy 205, three miles
northeast of Three Forks
1400 South 19th Street
Bozeman, Montana 59715
Tel: 406-994-4042
www.fwp.state.mt.us/parks/
parksreport.asp?mapnum=22

MONTANA, CONT'D

Clark's Lookout State Park
4200 Bannock Road
Dillon, Montana 59725
Tel: 406-834-3414
www.fwp.state.mt.us/parks/
parksreport.asp?mapnum=26

Travelers' Rest
Travelers' Rest State Park
6550 Mormon Creek Road
PO Box 995
Lolo, Montana 59847
Tel: 406-273-4253
www.travelersrest.org

Lolo Pass Visitor Center
Highway 12
Lolo, Montana 59847
Tel: 208-942-3113
http://visitmt.com/categories/more
info.asp?IDRRecordID=9525&SiteID=1

IDAHO

**Nez Perce National Historic Park
and Nez Perce Cultural Museum**
39063 U.S. Highway 95
Route 1, Box 100
Spalding, Idaho 83540-9715
Tel: 208-843-2261
www.nps.gov/nepe/

Sacajawea Interpretive Cultural and
Educational Center
200 Main Street
Salmon, Idaho 83467
Tel: 208-756-1188
www.sacajaweacenter.org

WASHINGTON

Alpowai Interpretive Center
Chief Timothy State Park
Highway 12
Clarkston, Washington 99403
Tel: 509-758-8613
www.parks.wa.gov/
parkpage.asp?selectedpark=
Chief%20Timothy&pageno=1

**Sacajawea State Park and
Interpretive Center**
2503 Sacajawea Park Road
Pasco, Washington 99301
Tel: 509-545-2361
www.parks.wa.gov/parkpage.asp?
selectedpark=Sacajawea&pageno=1

OREGON

Tamastslikt Cultural Institute
72789 Highway 331
Pendleton, Oregon 97801
Tel: 541-966-9748
www.tamastslikt.com

Columbia Gorge Discovery Center
Wasco County Historical Museum
5000 Discovery Drive
The Dalles, Oregon 97058
Tel: 541-296-8600
www.gorgediscovery.org

**Columbia Gorge Interpretive
Center Museum**
990 SW Rock Creek Drive
PO Box 396
Stevenson, Washington 98648
Tel: 800-991-2338
www.columbiagorge.org

**Bonneville Lock and
Dam Visitors Center**
PO Box 150
Cascade Locks, Oregon 97014
Tel: 541-374-8820 (Oregon)
509-427-4281 (Washington)
www.nwp.usace.army.mil/op/b/

Clark County Historical Museum
1511 Main Street
Vancouver, Washington 98661
Tel: 360-695-4681

Cape Disappointment State Park
(formerly Fort Canby State Park)
Highway 101
P.O. Box 488
Ilwaco, Washington 98624
Tel: 360-642-3078
www.parks.wa.gov/
parkpage.asp?selectedpark=
Cape%20Disappointment&pageno=1

Fort Clatsop National Memorial
92343 Fort Clatsop Road
Astoria, Oregon 97103
Tel: 503-861-2471
www.nps.gov/focl/

SELECTED REFERENCES AND RECOMMENDED FURTHER READING

Allen, John Logan. *Lewis and Clark and the Image of the American Northwest.* Dover Publications, 1975.

Ambler, Marjane, ed. *Tribal College Journal of American Indian Higher Education, vol. 14, no. 3.* American Indian Higher Education Consortium, Spring 2003.

Ambrose, Stephen E. *Undaunted Courage: Meriwether Lewis, Thomas Jefferson and the Opening of the American West.* Simon and Schuster, 1996.

Botkin, Daniel B. *Passage of Discovery: The American Rivers Guide to the Missouri River of Lewis and Clark.* Berkley Publishing Company, 1999.

Brokaw, Tom. *A Long Way from Home: Growing Up in the American Heartland.* Random House, 2002.

Cerami, Charles A. *Jefferson's Great Gamble: The Remarkable Story of Jefferson, Napoleon and the Men Behind the Louisiana Purchase.* Sourcebooks Trade, 2003.

Coonts, Stephen P. *The Cannibal Queen: A Flight Into the Heart of America.* Simon and Schuster, 1992.

Cutright, Paul Russell. *Lewis & Clark: Pioneering Naturalists.* University of Nebraska Press, 1969.

DeVoto, Bernard, ed. *The Journals of Lewis and Clark.* Houghton Mifflin, 1997.

Duncan, Dayton and Burns, Ken. *Lewis and Clark: The Journey of the Corps of Discovery: An Illustrated History.* Alfred A. Knopf, 2002.

Fifer, Barbara and Soderberg, Vicki. *Along the Trail with Lewis and Clark.* Montana Magazine, 1998.

Furtwangler, Albert. *Acts of Discovery: Visions of America in the Lewis and Clark Journals.* University of Illinois Press, 1993.

Hiebert, Carl. *Gift of Wings: An Aerial Celebration of Canada.* Boston Mills Press, 1995

Heat-Moon, William Least. *River Horse: The Logbook of a Boat Across America.* Houghton Mifflin, 1999.

Jones, Landon. *The Essential Lewis and Clark.* Ecco, 1999

Hunsaker, Joyce B. *Sacagawea Speaks: Beyond the Shining Mountains with Lewis and Clark.* Globe Pequot Press, 2001.

McHugh, Tom. *The Time of the Buffalo.* University of Nebraska Press, 1979.

Moulton, Gary E., ed. *Lewis, M. and Clark, W. The Journals of the Lewis and Clark Expedition.* 13 volumes. University of Nebraska Press, 1983-2001.

Norris, Kathleen. *Dakota: A Spiritual Geography.* Houghton Mifflin, 1993.

Peck, David J. *Or Perish in the Attempt: Wilderness Medicine in the Lewis and Clark Expedition.* Farcountry Press, 2002.

Phillips, H. Wayne. *Plants of the Lewis and Clark Expedition.* Mountain Press Publishing Company, 2003.

Raban, Jonathan. *Bad Land: An American Romance.* Pan Macmillan, 1996.

Ronda, James P. *Finding the West: Explorations with Lewis and Clark.* University of New Mexico Press, 2001.

Ronda, James P. *Lewis and Clark Among the Indians.* University of Nebraska Press, 1998.

Schmidt, Thomas. *National Geographic's Guide to the Lewis & Clark Trail.* The National Geographic Society, 1998.

Wagstaff, Patty. *Fire and Air.* Chicago Review Press, Inc. 1977.

Books in the *Roadside Geology Series* of the Mountain Press Publishing Company are available for South Dakota, the Lewis and Clark Trail in North Dakota, Montana, Idaho, Washington and Oregon.

Technical Notes

Building the Green "Canoe in the Sky"

When the military wants to create a plane that will do everything from zipping along at Mach 3, landing vertically and being invisible, all they have to do is throw billions of dollars at engineers and developers. In my case, however, everything started when an aircraft engineer I knew called one day and said he had an experimental kit plane that was perfect for the type of flying I like to do. After applauding him for the amazing performance specs he was telling me about, I simply put it in the back of my mind. Six months later, I ended up getting a test flight in that marvelous prototype plane. From that point on it went from the back of my mind to front and center. Even though I have very little interest in most aircraft, I became obsessed with this particular plane. Dreading the cost as well as the fact I had to build it, I still decided to become serial number 16 on the kit production line. Well, just like the military does things, my plane ended up way over budget and two years late.

Why I Call It "Cloud Chaser"

I've always had an intense fascination with clouds. Even as I stood on the ground, a giant thunderhead could hold my attention until it passed. How could people casually pass by with barely a glance at a 45,000-foot-high monster looming over their shoulder? When I finally freed my feet from the bonds of Mother Earth with an airplane, I headed straight for the clouds to photograph their many textures and life cycles. Like a pile of cotton balls in the palm of my hand, I could now view them with unlimited perspectives from the cockpit.

In the morning before the land was fully awake, the ground fog would slowly clump to form a string of soft beads above the river. Then the heat of the afternoon's solar energy would propel their moisture skyward faster than *Cloud Chaser* could climb. In late evening, their strength would slowly fade. Like a child holding a melting ice cream cone on a hot day, I would race around among them to get my shots before they could disappear into oblivion.

Playing on my obsession with clouds, I began using the shots of these nebulous things to create conceptual stock images. Building three-dimensional objects in the computer and combining them with my cloud pictures, I was successful in the stock photo business.

I am now able to pursue a new dream and explore new worlds with this fabulous ride up into the heavens, a plane named for those cumulus creatures—*Cloud Chaser.*

Plane Specs

On this trip, I logged almost 200 hours and 14,000 miles in my "tripod in the sky." In total, *Cloud Chaser* has logged over 860 hours.

Engines	two ROTAX 912s
Horsepower	100 each
Gross weight	1,054 lbs
Stall speed	38mph
Top speed	Mach .144
Cruise speed	50-80mph
Rate of climb	1,500 fpm
Solo, 50% fuel	2,000 fpm
Range	340 miles @70 mph
Endurance	6 hours
Landing roll	300 ft
Takeoff roll	less than 200 ft (all surfaces)

Photography Information

The camera I now use is a Canon 1Ds 11megapixel. The only two lenses I took on this trip were a 24-70 2.8 and 70-200 2.8. Even though I own a gyro stabilizer, it stayed at home. The extra grief of having to fight its resistance, the additional weight and lack of space in the cockpit outweighed its usefulness. Camera mounts don't work for me either. The way I fly and shoot, things happen too fast for anything other than handheld operation. Even though the camera is a major handfull, after weeks of flying and shooting, I got as comfortable as Wyatt Earp with his Colt 45. Shooting in weak twilight is most challenging because of having to work with slow shutter speeds.

Even simple things like changing lens filters while flying can get pretty exciting. One very bouncy day while trying to engage the finely-threaded filter to my lens, the plane hit a pothole in the sky causing the filter to suddenly leave my finger tips and float in front of my face instead of near my lap where the camera was. Quick reflexes saved the day. Because of this digital marvel—the camera—I can now start the photo editing process within minutes of parking the plane.

Behind the Scenes

Alan Lowery, Ron's older son who did most of the construction of Cloud Chaser. Much of the plane's parts came in plastic bags with paper labels. Who would ever thought that one of our greatest problems would be caused by those hateful cockroaches that would eat the ink off those labels?

"What is that weird blue light on top of your RV?" was a frequent question at campgrounds. The MotoSAT dish was installed days before we left by Tom Boggs. It provided our link to the outside world.

Mary's first solo in the "flying canoe."

Sue and Ron are watching the sunset at the airport in Arlington, Oregon.

"Road trip, road trip," Jack and Ryan exclaim.

Ron is training Jack to sit up like a prairie dog. The canine soon mastered that trick and showed off to the news media at every chance. Jack is such an odd mixture that curious people would frequently ask, "What kind of dog is that?" To give Jack a little dignity, Ron would reply, "Vox Weinerstein" while clicking his heels together. They would usually nod knowingly and reply, "That's interesting."

Windsock Media produces aviation adventure books.

Fine art prints of the photographs in this book are available.

For more information visit www.chasinglewisandclark.com

or call 423-344-3701.